Writing the
TEN-MINUTE
Play

Writing the
TEN-MINUTE
Play

*A Book for Playwrights and Actors
Who Want to Write Plays*

GLENN ALTERMAN

An Imprint of Hal Leonard Corporation

Published in 2013 by Limelight Editions
An Imprint of Hal Leonard Corporation
7777 West Bluemound Road
Milwaukee, WI 53213

Trade Book Division Editorial Offices
33 Plymouth St., Montclair, NJ 07042

Grateful Acknowledgment is made to the following for permission to reprint these plays.

On the Edge, by Craig Pospisil. Copyright 2005 by Craig Allan Pospisil. *On the Edge* was produced by the Vital Theater Company (Stephen Sunderlin, artistic director) in New York City as part of Vital Signs VIII on October 30, 2003. For permission to produce this play, contact Dramatists Play Service, 440 Park Avenue South, New York, NY 10016, www.Dramatists.com, postmaster@dramatists.com, 212-683-8960.

The Popcorn Sonata, by Jenny Lyn Bader. Used by permission of the author. For production rights, contact the playwright's representative, Jack Tantleff, Paradigm, 360 Park Avenue South, 16th Floor, New York, NY, 10010, jtantleff@paradigmagency.com.

The Pain in the Poetry, by Glenn Alterman. Used by permission of the author. For production rights, contact Playscripts, Inc. 450 Seventh Avenue, Suite 809, New York, NY, 10036, info@playscripts.com.

Printed in the United States of America
Book design by Publishers' Design and Production Services, Inc.

Library of Congress Cataloging-in-Publication Data is available upon request.
ISBN **978-1-55783-848-3**

www.limelighteditions.com

To the actors who have asked me over the years,
"How do you become a playwright?"

Contents

Acknowledgments   *xi*

Chapter 1: Before We Get Started   1

Who This Book Was Written For   1
Learning Playwriting from Many Sources   1
How I Wrote My First Play   2
Ten Ways to Get the Most out of This Book   4

Chapter 2: What Is a Ten-Minute Play?   7

The Ten-Minute Play: A Definition   7
When Did Ten-Minute Plays Begin?   7
Why Write a Ten-Minute Play?   8
Popularity of Ten-Minute Plays   8
Basic Rules for All Ten-Minute Plays   9

Chapter 3: Before Beginning Your Ten-Minute Play   11

Perking with an Idea   11
Deciding When to Begin   12
The Actor and the Playwright   13
As an Actor, Do I Have the Skills Necessary to Create My Own
Material?   13
Fear of Writing   14
Working Internally as an Actor and as a Writer   14

Techniques for Dealing with Writer's Block   15

Freewriting   16

Eleven Rules of Freewriting   16

Benefits of Freewriting   17

After You've Completed the Freewriting Session   17

Clustering (or Webbing): Finding the Initial Core of Your Work 17

How to Cluster   18

Starting Your Play with an Outline   19

Comparing Processes for Actors and Playwrights   19

Chapter 4: Playwriting Basics   **21**

Aristotle's *Poetics*   *22*

Freytag's Pyramid   24

Freytag's Five Dramatic Arcs   24

Chapter 5: Script Format   **25**

Chapter 6: Beginning Your Ten-Minute Play   **31**

How I Start My Ten-Minute Plays   31

Starting a Play with an Idea, a Theme, or an Image   33

Chapter 7: The Next Steps   **35**

Intention, Objective, and Action   35

The Setting and Time   36

The Best Way to Tell Your Story: The Play's Structure   36

Complications Arise   36

Realizing and Developing the Story of the Play   37

Actors Working on Their Plays   38

Ending the First Draft   38

Finding Your Title   39

After the First Draft   39

Chapter 8: Reading the First Draft   **41**

At What Point Should You Have Someone Else Read What
You've Written?   42

Selecting the Right Person to Read Your First Draft   42

The First Reading of Your Play   43

Cold Readings of Your Ten-Minute Play   43

Should You Be an Actor in the First Readings of Your
Ten-Minute Play?   44

Listening to Feedback and Comments   44

Not Allowing Others to Rewrite Your Play   44

Back to Rewrites   45

Chapter 9: Getting Your Play Out   **47**

E-mail Submissions   49

Actors: Should You Be in the First Production of Your Play?   49

Chapter 10: Interviews with Playwrights of Ten-Minute Plays   **51**

Jenny Lyn Bader   51

Don Nigro   56

Craig Pospisil   58

Mark Harvey Levine   62

Arlene Hutton   64

Alex Broun   67

Rich Orloff   69

Chapter 11: Interviews with Producers of Ten-Minute Plays   **73**

Kate Snodgrass   73

Alice Walker   75

Seth Gordon   78

Chapter 12: Interviews with Publishers of Ten-Minute Plays   **81**

Sarah Bernstein   81

Geri Albrecht   83

Lawrence Harbison   85

Chapter 13: Three Successful Ten-Minute Plays   89

    The Popcorn Sonata, Jenny Lyn Bader   89
    Discussion on Writing *The Popcorn Sonata*   98
    On the Edge, Craig Pospisil   102
    Creating *On the Edge*   113
    The Pain in the Poetry, Glenn Alterman   116
    Creating *The Pain in the Poetry*   123

Chapter 14: Where to Submit Your Ten-Minute Play   127

    Ten-Minute Play Festivals   128
    Publishers of Ten-Minute Plays   145

Chapter 15: Observations about the Ten-Minute Play   147

    Anastasia Traina, Playwright   147
    Scott C. Sickles, Artistic Director, WorkShop Theater Company,
    New York City   148
    Dirk Knef, Literary Advisor, After Folsom Festival
    (Berlin, Germany) and others   149
    Suzanne Bradbeer, Playwright   149
    Eduardo Arbo, Playwright, Barcelona   150
    Elaine Romero, Playwright   150

Chapter 16: And in the End   153

    Playwrights: Some Key Points to Remember   153
    Some Key Points for Actor/Playwrights   154

    Selected Bibliography   155

    About the Author   157

Acknowledgments

To all the actors that have performed in my ten-minute plays all over the world, and the directors who directed them, thank you.

To all the theater companies that produced my ten-minute plays in their ten-minute play festivals, thank you.

I'd like to personally thank Francine Tory for her tremendous help in putting this book together.

Thank you to all the playwrights, publishers, and producers who gave up their time and allowed me to interview them for this book. Your contribution is appreciated.

I'd also like to thank John Cerullo, Marybeth Keating, and all the folks at Limelight Editions for your help in the writing of this book.

Chapter 1

Before We Get Started

Who This Book Was Written For

I've written this book for playwrights (of all levels) who want to learn how to master the art of writing a ten-minute play. This book can be a valuable add-on to the knowledge you already have about writing plays. Writing a ten-minute play is more than just condensing a story. The form and demands are very specific, and even success as a playwright of full-length plays doesn't necessarily mean you can successfully write ten-minute plays. They're similar—but different.

This book is also written for actors who have never written a play. I was, and still am, an actor. As you'll discover in my bio, I more or less fell into playwriting. It all began with writing my first ten-minute play. In this book I guide actors through the process of learning how to write a ten-minute play, beginning with the skills, knowledge, and experience you already have as an actor. Actors may discover, as I did, that it's really not that far a stretch from being an actor to writing plays. The ten-minute play is one of the best ways to learn about playwriting.

And finally, this book is for those people who have never written a play, but always wanted to. The ten-minute play is a great way to start. I've included basic information on playwriting that should be helpful to you.

Learning Playwriting from Many Sources

Over the years I have taken several playwriting classes and joined several playwriting groups. One thing that I've learned is that the craft of writing plays, whether it's a ten-minute play or a full-length, can be approached from many points of view. It is not an exact science. What I've attempted to do in this book is to distill much of the information I've learned over the years about playwriting from my personal experiences, from playwriting classes, from the books I've read on playwriting, from discussions with successful ten-minute playwrights, and from producers of ten-minute play festivals.

My goal was to get as many points of view on this subject as possible. You'll notice that in some of the interviews there are similar responses to the interview questions, while in others there are different ones. I'll let you, the reader, judge which answers are the most helpful to you.

When I was a young actor I studied with many of the great acting teachers in New York, from Stella Adler to Mira Rostova, Terry Schreiber, Michael Howard, Wynn Handman, Larry Moss, and on and on. I loved studying and learning about the craft of acting. I learned different things from each of the teachers. Similarly, I want this book to show you the many approaches there are to writing the ten-minute play (or any play).

How I Wrote My First Play

About forty years ago I was a working actor. I performed in plays, in theater, and on TV. About thirty years ago I became a writer: first a monologue writer, then a book writer, and then a playwright.

Like many actors, I was always looking for new monologues for auditions. It was a tiresome process. Each monologue that I'd find seemed to have something wrong with it, something that eliminated it from my being able to use it for auditions. It was a very frustrating situation. I was constantly monologue-hunting when I could have been better spending my time looking for acting work.

One day, on a whim—well, actually out of total frustration—I decided to try to write my own monologue. Considering that I had no background in creative writing, I knew it was going to be a challenge. After all those years of monologue hunting, I certainly knew what I wanted. The monologue that I was going to write would have a beginning, middle, and end; a conflict of some kind; and a character that interested me, one I could identify with. But, most importantly, it had to have a good yarn, an engaging story.

It was trial and error for quite a while. But one thing I gradually began to realize was that I could use my acting skills to help me write monologues. Some of the same skills that I'd used as an actor to create characters in plays, I also could use to create characters in monologues. After a few very long, trying weeks I completed my first monologue. I felt a tremendous sense of achievement.

I was studying acting at that time with Wynn Handman in New York. When I brought my new monologue to class one night and nervously performed it, it went over very well. Everyone wanted to know where I had found this great new monologue. And so it began: I started writing monologues for the other actors in the class. This went on for months. At each class someone would be performing one of my monologues. The more I wrote, the more I realized I was on to something. I started to develop more efficient ways of working. I learned more from my mistakes than from my successes.

At the end of that first year I had completed over a hundred and twenty-five monologues (not to mention the dozens of discarded ones). I was now what I considered officially a "monologue writer." My monologues became very popular around the New York theater scene, and eventually my first book of original monologues, *Street Talk: Character Monologues for Actors*, was published by Smith & Kraus. The book was quite successful. Without making a long story longer, many books of original monologues followed, and then many theater-related books. Somehow I had gone from being a monologue writer to being a book writer.

It was during this prolific period of monologue and book writing that I decided to attempt writing a play. It seemed that ten-minute play festivals were turning up everywhere, and I just wanted to see if I could write one. As with the monologues, I'd never written a play before, had never even thought about it. But I realized: I'm an actor, I've been in plays, how hard could it be? So I decided to attempt writing a ten-minute play.

I'd heard you should "write about what you know." So I wrote a two-character play about these two guys, best friends in Brooklyn (where I grew up). I figured I'd just let them "talk." I'd heard from other playwrights that the best way to write a play is to set up your characters in a specific place and let them speak to each other. I wasn't sure exactly what that meant, but I gave it a go. Well, the play seemed to write itself. I let my imagination be the ringmaster. After some cuts and rewrites, my first ten-minute play, *Goin' Round on Rock Solid Ground*, was born. When it became a finalist at the prestigious Actors Theatre of Louisville's Ten-Minute Play Competition, I was hooked. I was now a playwright.

Since then, I've written dozens of ten-minute plays, short plays, full-lengths, and screenplays. I've been lucky enough to win many awards, and have had many productions in the United States and in Europe. There's no doubt in my mind that luck came into all this, but, to some degree, so did craft. And of course being proactive about getting my plays out there.

Ten Ways to Get the Most out of This Book

1. This book is written for experienced playwrights, beginning playwrights, actors, and just about anyone who ever wanted to write a ten-minute play. If you wish, you can read the book from cover to cover, but it may not be necessary for the first read.

2. I suggest that you first look through the Table of Contents; see what stands out. Look for those things that interest you at the present time, that pertain to your specific situation. Then skim through the book, stopping at those chapters that you feel are of interest to you right now. For instance, if you've never written a play, I suggest you read Chapters 4 and 5, which deal with playwriting technique and proper playwriting format. If you're an experienced playwright, these chapters may be of interest just to review; or you may wish to skip them for now.

3. After you've read through the particular chapters that apply to you, I suggest that you THEN read through the entire book, taking notes or highlighting those things that you find apply to your particular situation. Experienced playwrights, you can skip some of the basics, unless you want to review them.

4. As you begin working on your ten-minute play, you may want to refer to the sections in Chapter 3 that help you in getting started. If you're not sure how to start writing or feel blocked, I recommend that you specifically read and do the freewriting and clustering exercises.

5. If you get stuck at any point as you are writing your play, refer back to earlier chapters to see where you might have gone off track, or how to continue when you've hit a wall.

6. During the rewrites, or even after the first draft of your ten-minute play, you may find some inspiration in rereading some of the experiences of other playwrights, producers of ten-minute play festivals, and publishers of ten-minute plays.

7. Once you've finished reading the entire book, put the information you've learned to practical use. You can then use this book as a checklist while working on your play.

8. This book is meant as a starting point, a launching pad for your ten-minute play. Refer to it as often as you need to.

9. Depending on your playwriting experience, you may not feel the need to apply every rule in this book. If something you've learned prior to reading this book still works for you, continue using it. But always leave room for the possibility of discovering new ways to add on to what has worked for you in the past.

10. My purpose in writing this book was not only to instruct, but to inspire. The point of the book, the reason I wrote it, was to encourage you, whether you're a beginning playwright, an experienced playwright, an actor with no playwriting experience, or someone who's never written a play. Whether you aspire to write short plays, one-acts, or full-lengths, this book is designed to help you get your start. Good luck.

Chapter 2

What Is a Ten-Minute Play?

The Ten-Minute Play: A Definition

A ten-minute play is a play that when produced on a stage lasts ten minutes. Now, that seems simple enough, right? Usually one page of dialogue and stage directions equals about a minute of stage action. Just to be certain, you should always have a couple of informal readings after you've done a draft of your ten-minute play to verify that it runs ten minutes.

A ten-minute play is not a sketch. It is a very short play that has a beginning, middle, and end. The more successful ones are light on exposition and strong on setting up a conflict, and have characters that are established almost immediately. Each of the characters in the ten-minute play (and hopefully there won't be too many) should have his or her own arc. Your characters should start off at one place and end up in a different place at the end of the play. Hopefully, there should also be some surprises along the way.

Many playwrights write plays that are longer than ten minutes and then attempt to fool producers and publishers by making the font size very small, creating large margins, or single-spacing the dialogue. Don't. Producers and publishers are on to you. A ten-minute play plays ten minutes on the stage—end of story.

When Did Ten-Minute Plays Begin?

You could say the ten-minute play goes back to 1923, when Pierre Loving published a book of ten-minute plays by such renowned playwrights as August Strindberg, Arthur Schnitzler, and Ferenc Molnar. No one is certain whether these playwrights were specifically asked to write ten-minute plays for this anthology or already had them in their collections.

Real interest in ten-minute plays, however, began in 1978 at the Actors Theatre of Louisville, where Jon Jory was the producing director. Mr. Jory wanted to give beginning as well as well-known writers an opportunity to participate at his theater. Some of the writers that wrote plays for that early festival were Douglas Turner Ward, Lanford Wilson, Israel Horowitz, Marsha Norman, and John Guare. The theme that the playwrights were instructed to write about at that first festival was "Holidays."

Many of today's top playwrights, from David Mamet to Tony Kushner to Christopher Durang, have written ten-minute plays.

Why Write a Ten-Minute Play?

Ten-minute plays can be both incredibly easy and incredibly difficult to write. On the one hand, you don't have all the multiple subplots, the abundance of characters, the many scenes, etc., of a full-length play. But you still have to create a story with a beginning, middle, and end; believable characters; dramatic tension; and a story that makes theatrical sense. If nothing else it's a wonderful exercise in learning how to condense a story to its most important elements. It's a way to learn how to write concise, "only what must be said" dialogue that moves a story rapidly to a conclusion.

Popularity of Ten-Minute Plays

Ten-minute play festivals have become increasingly popular with theaters over the last few years for several reasons. Perhaps with the popularity of the Internet, music videos, and television, full-length plays are not quite as much in demand as they once were. There was a time when if you went to the theater it wasn't unusual to see a play that ran two and a half to three hours with two intermissions. Those plays are produced far less frequently today. Another reason ten-minute play festivals are very popular today is that they're relatively inexpensive to produce. Because the festivals present a group of plays, the set must be simple and flexible, and props kept to a minimum.

Yet another reason is that ten-minute play festivals get larger audiences because there are so many writers, actors, and directors involved. Everyone involved will invite their friends and colleagues to see their work.

One final thing to think about is that writing a ten-minute play can be a great way to introduce yourself to a theater or theater company.

Successfully submitting your ten-minute play to their festival means an opportunity for you to introduce them to your work, whether you usually write one-acts or full-length plays.

Basic Rules for All Ten-Minute Plays

What follows are some basic rules to keep in mind before starting a ten-minute play, some essentials that many successful ten-minute plays have in common. We'll look first at tips on structuring your play, then at suggestions specifically oriented toward getting your play selected for performance in a festival. As with any art, not all the rules must always apply.

Writing Your Best Ten-Minute Play

- Make sure the conflict in your play is strong and immediate. The sooner you set up the conflict, the better.
- Make sure your play has a conflict and isn't merely an argument between characters.
- If you can set up obstacles along the way that can be believably resolved in ten minutes, by all means do.
- Some sources suggest finding a metaphor and revising your play around that metaphor.
- Every detail in your play should relate to the action of the play.
- Try to keep your cast small. In a ten-minute period you really don't have much time to develop many characters. In general, you don't want to have more than three characters in your play.
- Each of your characters should be very different from the others. Since you probably will only be dealing with a few characters, this shouldn't be too difficult.
- Your characters and story should be believable. I know this may seem obvious, but even in a surreal play we need to have a scenario and characters that we, the audience, can somehow identify with.
- You characters should all have very clear goals (i.e., what they want). They should have different goals from one another.
- You don't want to have characters entering and exiting all the time; it can get too busy.
- Keep your exposition to a minimum. You want your characters to say what they have to say without getting into long-winded stories or monologues. Most ten-minute plays are dialogue driven. Don't

feel you need to tell your audience what to think. Just show them why to think it.

- If you can show it, there's no need to talk about it.
- Try not to telegraph the ending of your play too early. If we can figure out the ending too quickly, we miss the fun of taking the journey.
- You must be certain that the ending of the play resolves itself in a way that is believable. I'm all for twist/surprise endings, but make sure that the action of your play earns it. There is nothing more frustrating for an audience member than to see a play with an ending that's not justified. They'll feel duped, that they wasted their ten minutes.
- Every detail you've set up in the course of your ten-minute play must come together and pay off at the end; otherwise your audience will feel shortchanged.

Getting Your Ten-Minute Play Performed

- I've read in several ten-minute play guidelines that the play should be between 1500 and 1700 words. I'm not quite sure if that's always the case, but it should give you a sense of what some theaters expect, and can be used as a gauge.
- Keep stage directions to a minimum. They take up valuable space in your script.
- Keep your props and costumes to a minimum.
- Keep your set simple. You don't want to create an elaborate set that requires time to set up and break down. Remember, ten-minute play festivals want to be able to move smoothly and quickly from one play to the next.
- Try not to have too many technical requirements for your play (i.e., sound, light cues, etc.). Remember, your play is just one of many in an evening of ten-minute plays. The lighting and sound designers need to do many evenings' worth of cues. Try not to overburden them with too many cues for just your play. Too many cues could prevent your play from being selected for production.
- Make sure your play is ten minutes long. Before you send out any ten-minute play, have several readings of it to be **sure** it's ten minutes; end of story!

Chapter 3

Before Beginning Your Ten-Minute Play

If you've never written a play of any kind, writing a ten-minute play can be a great way to start. If you've written plays before, but have never written a ten-minute play, this book can be a lesson in learning how to condense and tell stories in a concise manner.

In the next couple of chapters I'll be discussing writing the ten-minute play from my experience. I am in no way saying that my way is the only way to write a ten-minute play. Every playwright, every artist, creates in his or her own particular way. First I'll tell how I write ten-minute plays, and then later in the book you'll see how other playwrights write theirs.

Perking with an Idea

All plays begin with an idea, a topic, an issue, a story line, a line of dialogue, or even an image that engages your mind. Perhaps you've had an idea for a piece and don't yet know how you want to express it. Sometimes it's better not to do anything for a while. Just let it percolate ("perk"). Many artists talk about an initial gestation period before they do any actual work on a new piece. This is different from a delay tactic for avoiding work. By ruminating you allow your subconscious mind to collect the necessary information for you. Think of the process as the work of little elves who magically know how to gather and organize the material you've been looking for. Let them do the work for you. You'll find these elves even more helpful later on if you get stuck.

Speaking of getting stuck, this can happen at any time while working on a play. When I find myself stuck when beginning or while working on any new play, I generally put the play away for a period of time and focus on other things, letting those elves figure out how I can get "unstuck." It always amazes me how, when I come back to that same play with a fresh mind, the problems, the block, seems to disappear and the solution seems apparent. There is an aha moment and I feel unstuck.

So when you feel ready to start, when the idea has perked—start, and let the writing move at its own pace.

Also, you may want to look at your dreams and keep a journal during this time.

Deciding When to Begin

The right time to begin writing your ten-minute play is when you feel ready, motivated. Before starting, make sure you have enough time to create and explore. If you have an appointment in an hour, now may not be the best time. You want to feel relaxed, not rushed.

Beginning means sitting in front of your computer or taking out that writing pad and seeing what comes to you. Whether you write on a computer or initially on a notepad is up to you. For many years I wrote my plays out longhand. Then, when they were at a developed place, I'd type them out on the computer. These days I go right to the computer and start.

You don't have to begin with characters speaking dialogue. As a matter of fact, you can start by recording any thoughts of frustration that you may be feeling sitting there. Write it! (See "Free Writing" and "Clustering," next chapter.) Whatever blockage you may be feeling, express it in words. Thoughts like "Damn it, this isn't working!" or "I have nothing to say!" or whatever's going through your mind at the moment, put it down on paper or type it on your computer.

Sometimes a line of dialogue, something you heard someone say that day, or even an image is all you need to begin. Write down whatever it is and see if it conjures up something more for you. Perhaps the character who is saying that particular line will start to take shape in your imagination. Maybe you'll get a sense of the type of person who's saying this line. Or you may see an image, a face, even a person you know or knew.

After writing down that initial line, you want to get a response to that line from another character. Again, let your imagination take over; don't try to "figure out what should come next." Trust your instincts and let 'er rip. Jot down the response line; see where that takes you. Hopefully what follows is an entire riff or sequence of dialogue, opening up the play for you. Just go with it. Write the lines down and keep out of the way.

If nothing else seems to follow that first line, just leave it on the page and come back to it when something does. There's no need to pressure yourself or force something when nothing's coming. The impetus, the idea may open up at another time when your imagination is ready to move forward with your play. Or it may start filling in when you're doing something entirely different, like washing the dishes or jogging. I'll say more about the way I allow a first line to lead me into a play, and about dealing with writer's block, later on. (See "Techniques for Dealing with Writer's Block When Starting a Play")

The Actor and the Playwright

Generally, actors interpret and perform what a playwright has written. The actor's creative life involves constant collaboration with other artists (the director, other actors, etc.) early on in a play's production. The writer starts out creating alone; only after completing a play does he or she collaborate with the play's production team (producer, director, actors, etc.). Yet the interconnectedness of both professions should be obvious. The most evident similarity between the actor and the writer is that both are creative artists, and both use their imagination in their work. We'll be looking at techniques that draw on these key characteristics and merge both of these professions in writing your ten-minute play.

As an Actor, Do I Have the Skills Necessary to Create My Own Material?

I personally feel that almost anyone can write, tell stories, and maybe even write plays. If you've had experiences, you have stories like no one else's. Your stories are unique, yours alone. How you'll tell your stories is as individual as you. Your imagination is also unique to you.

A few years ago I was a mentor at the Edward Albee Theatre Conference (now called the Last Frontier Theatre Conference) in Valdez, Alaska. There was a play that year, very imaginative and deeply moving, that stood out. It was written by a fourteen-year-old girl who had *never seen a play*. She had read only one or two plays in her whole life. But this play was something she wanted, needed to write. The results were magical. She wrote not just a good play, but a *great* play.

Actors have an advantage over many first-time playwrights, since acting in plays means you are constantly reading plays and probably know more than you think about structure, dialogue, format. Once you begin writing a play of your own, you may find that you know "instinctively" what to do. And there's no reason why you as an actor can't take a playwriting class or two, whether to bolster your knowledge or your confidence in what you may already know.

Fear of Writing

There is always the fear that if you expose yourself in your writing, your audience will sit in judgment of you and your life. This is true of all artists, including actors. You can't be too preoccupied by this. You can never second-guess an audience, so why waste time worrying about the people you're writing for? If you honestly find that you have something to say that is engaging, interesting, or funny to you, put it down on paper or type it on the computer. You may be surprised to find that it will resonate for others, too.

Working Internally as an Actor and as a Writer

Many actors in America are trained in internal or psychological acting techniques. The Actors Studio, using the "method technique," bases a great deal of the work on the actor's personal life and inner responses to the character he or she is working on. Any of the many books by Constantin Stanislavski about "the system" (which later became known as "the method"), or acting books by Lee Strasberg or Stella Adler, offer excellent exercises that actors and writers may find helpful in developing characters for their ten-minute plays. After using some of the method techniques and exercises, you can combine what you discover with some improvisation work and imagination. By using your own memories, and then adding your imagination to the stew, you can create all sorts of characters in interesting situations. Writers working this way aren't working just conceptually, but from inner experiences and memories.

Improvisation is a great way to free your imagination and develop plays. Many actors are already adept at improvisation, so this way to develop your scripts might be an easy stepping-stone from acting to playwriting. British film director Mike Leigh is well known for developing his films (*Naked*, *Life Is Sweet*, and others) by working improvisationally with the actors and developing the script from their improvisations. Playwright Jeffrey Sweet is a big advocate of developing plays improvisationally. If you'd like to explore working this way on your ten-minute plays, check out his books, *Something Wonderful Right Away: An Oral History of the Second City* and *Solving Your Script: Tools and Techniques for the Playwright*.

Sometimes our creativity feels like a blocked exhaust pipe. And the harder we try to force the smoke out, the worse it seems to get. We are plagued with doubts and negative thoughts such as "Who's going to care about this?" "Am I, is it, really good enough?" All artists deal with doubts all the time. I'm sure that you've dealt with them as an actor. Eventually you learn to live with creative doubts. You'll realize that self-censoring and insecurities are just part of the creative process.

One solution to the problem of writer's block is to realize that to get "there" (wherever it is you're hoping to go, creatively) you have to start with "here." And "here" is the room that you're in, with nothing on that paper. You have to allow and accept the present moment. "Okay, I'm blocked, I've got nothing." Use that as the launching pad and see if that admission gets the motor going.

An image that's been used to describe being creatively blocked is that of rocks in front of a cave. It may feel as if huge boulders are blocking your way into some magical creative cave. If only I could get behind those rocks, you think, I just know there's some good creative stuff inside that cave. Sometimes those rocks blocking the creative entranceway are, themselves, pure creative gold, the very stuff you've been looking for. But you didn't realize it, couldn't see their value. They are the starting point! What I'm saying is start where you are. Start in the exact moment/place of your frustration or anger. What does that feeling do to you? What does it look like, how does it sound? Put it into words, write it down, put it into the characters you're trying to create.

Techniques for Dealing with Writer's Block

Some writers, when experiencing writer's block, say that just writing anything, even copying a page out of a book, can help them get back into the groove of writing.

Some playwrights, when feeling blocked, go out and see another playwright's work. They say that just being in a theater and seeing good material can be quite inspiring.

Keeping a pad with you at all times to jot down a thought or line of dialogue can also be helpful (or keep notes on your iPad, smartphone, etc.). An idea may come to you during any part of your day—while walking, on a bus, in the shower, anywhere. One strong thought or image or some great line of dialogue can be just the trigger that will get you started.

After actually starting a play, I know of some playwrights that end each day's work in the middle of a sentence or thought. When they return the next day they can pick up the thread of where they left off and not have to look at an empty page.

Freewriting

Freewriting is a great way to get started writing a new ten-minute play. Several playwrights I spoke with said that on occasion it's helped them get over a bad case of writer's block. Freewriting is a method by which you put your pen to paper and write nonstop for at least ten minutes. It's a method for generating new ideas. With this method you allow ideas to lead you (rather than the other way around). When it's working well, one idea will ignite another. This method is about quantity, not quality. It's about first thoughts, impulses, anything that comes to mind. Quite often we squelch our impulses. This exercise helps you free yourself from that tendency.

Eleven Rules of Freewriting

1. Write as quickly as you can.
2. Write without boundaries.
3. Don't stop to censor or revise anything.
4. Don't stop to figure out what you've written; don't analyze it.
5. Don't attempt to think or get logical about the words you've written.
6. Don't pay any attention to spelling, grammar, or punctuation.
7. Write all over the page. Don't be concerned about margins or even the lines on the page.
8. If you can't think of anything to write, then write about that.
9. Don't cross out anything you've written.

10. Even if something comes up for you that is embarrassing, painful, or frightening, write it down.
11. Take a sentence from what you've written, put it on the top of a page, then write for ten minutes about that sentence, using it as a topic sentence.

Benefits of Freewriting

Freewriting instills discipline. It's a productive way to work through fears and anxieties about creating new material. Some writers use this method as a daily warm-up exercise before starting work on their piece. Or, when you're working under pressure, it can jump-start you into your day's work. Freewriting is a useful tool that can give you ideas and help you learn to write effortlessly, more spontaneously. It can help to turn off that self-censoring device that can be destructive, especially in the early stages of starting a play.

After You've Completed the Freewriting Session

Remember, this exercise is about process, not product. After you've done your freewriting session, look through the material to see if there is anything that you can use (a word, a phrase, some dialogue) for the play that you're about to get started on or are presently working on. If there is, save it. Then immediately get rid of the rest of the freewriting work that you've done. The reason you do this is that sometimes there's a tendency to want to revise what you already have on the page, using it as a first draft. That's not the idea of this exercise. It's not a first draft; it's the starting point for what will (hopefully) become your new play.

Clustering (or Webbing): Finding the Initial Core of Your Work

Following the freewriting exercise, I suggest another excellent exercise called "clustering." Clustering is a very popular writing method that was created by Gabriele Lusser Rico and discussed in her book *Writing the Natural Way*, an excellent book for writers. Her technique helps you focus on what you're trying to say in your work. It utilizes the right side of the brain's ability to organize information. Sometimes when we start out on a new piece it may be difficult to determine which areas of our work we need to focus on. Clustering helps you to find the throughline to your work. It helps you to zero in when too many thoughts and ideas seem to blur your creative landscape. Ironically it's also useful when there's a lack of ideas. Like freewriting, which it's similar to, this technique helps you to bypass your conscious mind and get to your unconscious. The best way to describe clustering is "total free association" or "brainstorming."

How to Cluster

Start this exercise with a fresh sheet of paper. Write a word that is somehow connected to the ten-minute play that you're about to start work on. Don't be concerned about which word you choose; whatever word comes to mind will be fine. If you don't have a play in mind, any word that comes to mind is the one to start with.

- Place the word in the middle of the page. Circle the word. Look at it for a moment. This core word or nucleus is the jumping-off point for the exercise.
- Now, as quickly as you can, allow yourself to free-associate around your nucleus word: write whatever thoughts, words, images, or phrases come to you, uncensored, as many as you can. Each new word or phrase that you write down should radiate out from the nucleus word.
- Draw circles around each new word or phrase. Use each one as a new starting point to which you link further related ideas, phrases, bits of dialogue, etc., as they arise in your mind. You can add arrows indicating direction if you wish.
- If nothing spills out, doodle, putting arrows on your existing cluster. The doodling allows your hand to keep moving and may allow for possible associations.
- Don't waste time trying to analyze anything; just go with your gut feelings. Don't stop until you have exhausted all possibilities. Keep going until you feel the need to write something. This shift will come in a thought like "I've got it! I know what I want to write!"
- Most writers work with clusters for up to a few minutes. When you feel compelled to write, start immediately! Don't allow your

inhibitions to hold you back. Free-associate, write with abandon, let your imagination go. Start writing as fast as you can.

- If nothing particular inspires you to write, then look at the words or phrases in the cluster and select any one of them. Start writing about that word or phrase. It may give rise to dialogue, images, or even new plot ideas. Keep writing for at least ten minutes if you can. You can refer back to the cluster if you wish.
- Remember, there is no right or wrong here. This is only an exercise. Don't force it.

Starting Your Play with an Outline

Some playwrights like to start their plays with an outline. The outline can serve as a sort of skeletal script, giving the writer a sense of direction for the piece. They start off with a cast of characters. Then they invent ways for these characters to interact at different points in their lives. Hopefully a plot emerges out of these interactions.

Some playwrights' outlines are only a paragraph long, while others go on for pages. With a ten-minute play, the outline will obviously be much shorter than for a full-length. I've written a few ten-minute plays using outlines. It's not my favorite way to work, but it has worked. I know many playwrights that only work this way. I personally like to let my subconscious imagination run wild when starting new plays. I don't care for any preset ideas or borders. But whichever way works for you is the way to go. You might try both ways: start with an outline if you like, and then try freewriting.

Comparing Processes for Actors and Playwrights

Actors generally come to a first read of a new play with no preconceived ideas of who their character will be, or how they will go about creating him or her. It's a very vulnerable time in an actor's creative process. It's a time of taking in, reading the script, digesting information, and then preparing to respond creatively to what you've read.

After that initial reading of the play, you have feelings and ideas about the character you are about to create. Creative juices are flowing; the imagination is at work. Starting with some initial impulses, you begin thinking of ways of ways to create your new character.

At the beginning of writing a new play, you, the writer, are opening a door for yourself. From the very first lines you write, you are taking yourself somewhere, although you may not be quite sure where yet. The more spontaneous you can allow yourself to be, the more personal and original your work will be. In this way, both the actor and the writer begin at the same place. It's a place of unknowing. It can be a frightening moment or an exciting one, like the moment just before you board a roller coaster. Trust yourself and let the ride surprise you!

Chapter 4

Playwriting Basics

As you write your ten-minute play, you will find it useful to know certain basic points of playwriting. I believe that the information in this chapter will be especially helpful to those who have never written a play before, although experienced playwrights may find it informative, too. What follows are some rules that apply to all plays, long and short.

- Conflict—Conflict is the essence of a play. The stronger the conflict, the more engaging your play will be. Character one wants something. Character two will do everything in his or her power to block character one from getting it. When that happens, we have conflict. Weak conflicts make for boring plays. Make the stakes high and you have a good chance of creating an engaging play.
- Character—Characters are the people who populate your play. Their personalities, their history, and their desires are expressed in the dialogue; i.e., what the characters say to each other. Your characters want something; in acting terms that's called "intention." Actors are taught that by discovering what the character needs you'll discover how you might play the character. The way the characters speak, what their lives are like, their family, and most importantly what they want, should all be taken into account when making playing choices.
- The Protagonist—This is the main character we will be following in your play, the one who wants something and runs into a conflict in attempting to get it. As in life, not all protagonists get what they want. Sometimes they discover that that pot of gold they've desperately been seeking is not at all what they thought it would be. It's how the character evolves in the play that is most interesting, the journey, so to speak. The character should be different at the end of

the play than at the beginning. The knowledge the protagonist gains during the play changes him or her. The challenges, the obstacles that the protagonist overcomes (or doesn't) help to determine how he or she will change. Self-awareness comes from overcoming or attempting to overcome the challenges and obstacles.

- The Antagonist—To create conflict you must have an antagonist, or opposing force: something or someone must get in the way of the protagonist, blocking his or her path toward the goal. The antagonist can be another character in the play, an event, or an obstacle confronting the protagonist. The two forces going up against each other create the conflict in the play. The stronger the conflict of these two opposing forces, the more interesting your play will be.

- Stage Directions—These are the instructions a playwright includes in the script to let the actors and the director know what action is occurring during the scene. The best advice I can give is to use them as little as possible. Just include specific actions that must be addressed to make the play work efficiently. Some playwrights include way too many stage directions; save that for your screenplays.

- Setting—This is where and when your play takes place. It may include the furniture you must have in the scene or a doorway or window if needed. The setting may also be an indicator of the style of the play you're writing. Remember that this is theater, and try to keep it simple. Don't create scenes or sets that are not stage worthy. Some beginning writers create elaborate sets and scenes that might work better in film than on the stage. Again, with the ten-minute play, less is more. If your play is part of a ten-minute play festival, having too much furniture will impede moving on to the next play after yours is over. On some occasions plays have not been selected, or are eliminated from ten-minute play festivals, because of their set requirements.

Aristotle's *Poetics*

The Greek philosopher Aristotle (384–322 B.C.E.) wrote two books on aesthetics: *The Poetics* and *Rhetoric*. *The Poetics* is the earliest work of dramatic theory and originally addressed both comedy and tragedy, though the book on comedy has been lost. The surviving book deals with tragedy, which Aristotle felt was the "most refined version of poetry dealing with lofty ideals."

While the following information on dramatic theory is highly condensed, it may serve as a starting point for those who wish to read further;

and I believe some of this information may be of use in creating your ten-minute play.

Aristotle believed tragedy should be mimetic (a good imitation), serious, and a good length; that it should contain rhythm and harmony; and that the rhythm and harmony should appear in various combinations as the story evolved. He believed that tragedy was meant to be performed, not narrated, and that through catharsis it should purge feelings of pity and fear that had been aroused earlier in the telling of the story.

In his *Poetics*, Aristotle said that unified plot structure is formed like a triangle. It begins with the *protasis*, or the introduction, in the lower left-hand corner of the triangle. The highest point of the triangle is called the *epitasis*, or middle, which is the crisis, and in the lower right-hand corner of the triangle is the resolution of the conflict, which he called the *catastrophe*.

Aristotle broke down tragedy into six elements: plot, character, thought, diction, melody and spectacle.

- **Plot.** The plot should have a beginning that isn't a consequence of any previous action, a middle that grows logically from the beginning, and an end that logically flows from the middle and from which "no further action should necessarily follow." All the scenes in a play should be linked together by "probability and necessity."
- **Character.** The character supports the plot; in other words, the characters' personal motivation will impact the cause and effect chain of action. These events should create "pity and fear in the audience." The protagonist, who Aristotle felt should be well respected and wealthy, changes due to "a great error" or "a frailty in his character." Each character in a play should have a distinct personality, age, appearance, beliefs, socioeconomic background, and language.
- **Thought.** While Aristotle doesn't explain what he means by this term, he does say that "speeches should reveal character."
- **Diction** is "the expression of the meaning in words" that are proper and appropriate to the plot, characters, and end of the tragedy. Here Aristotle discusses the stylistic elements of tragedy, particularly metaphor. The ability to use metaphors, he believed, implied "an eye for resemblance" that was crucial in dramatic art.
- **Melody.** Aristotle saw the chorus as an actor in the play that should be fully integrated into the story.
- **Spectacle** is everything that is seen and heard during the play: costumes, scenery, and even special effects. Aristotle felt however, that

it was the job of the playwright, and not the stage machinist, to move the audience to emotion.

Freytag's Pyramid

Gustav Freytag (1816–1895), a German critic and novelist, modified Aristotle's triangle, adding two additional elements. The first was the *complication*, which is a rising action, ascending from the lower left-hand corner to the higher middle of the triangle. The *falling action* he placed descending from the highest middle to the lowest right-hand corner of the triangle. He used all five elements to analyze the structure of drama, calling them *dramatic arcs*. Freytag's pyramid can be useful as a guide while when you're working on any plays of any length.

Freytag's Five Dramatic Arcs

- **Introduction (or Exposition)**—This is when we first meet the characters of the play. It's when the protagonist and antagonist are introduced and the play's conflict begins to reveal itself. We see where the play takes place, and the time and mood of the piece. During this initial arc we get some sense of how the characters interconnect in the play.
- **Rising Action**—During this arc things start to perk. The conflict becomes more apparent, and at this point we should be feeling the tension. Obstacles may appear, further blocking the protagonist from his goal.
- **Climax**—This is the point in the play where things dramatically change. Depending on the play you've written, they can get better or worse. This is the highest point in the pyramid.
- **Falling Action**—A resolution begins to appear in the conflict between our protagonist and antagonist. Generally the protagonist will either win or lose to his or her foe in this dramatic arc. It is here that we see that the climax or the main action is over and the story of the play starts to come to its conclusion.
- **Conclusion**—Sometimes called the catastrophe, this arc is the end of the play's story. In some plays the protagonist achieves his or her goal, as so often happens in comedies. When this doesn't happen, then quite often what we have is a tragedy. The conflict that we set up should now be resolved.

Chapter 5

Script Format

Up to this point in the book we've been looking at exercises to stimulate ideas and touched on classic playwriting structure theory. As the following chapters take you through the actual writing of your ten-minute play, it will be helpful to know the preferred format for theatrical scripts.

Below is the proper format for your ten-minute play. Some playwrights use the format they see in play anthology books. This is not the correct format for your plays.

- Your title page should be formatted correctly (see sample page). Make sure the title of your play is centered and all in caps. Beneath that you want to identify it as a ten-minute play (not in caps). Your name should be below that (unless you are submitting to a competition that requests that you leave your name off the script and place it instead on a separate information page).
- The dialogue in your play begins 1.5 inches from the left side of your page.
- Character names are always in caps.
- Any stage actions are indented 3 inches from the left and should be enclosed in parentheses.
- The dialogue of your play should be single-spaced.
- Use capital letters to bring the reader's attention to special design effects, such as sound and lights. For example: LIGHTS: Bright sunlight shines through the kitchen window.
- Directions for actors—i.e., specific instructions you'd like the actor playing the role to follow—should be placed directly below the character's name, in parenthesis. For instance, *(Crying)* or *(Loudly)*.
- If a character's speech begins at the end of one page with just one line and continues onto the next page, it's best to move the entire

speech to the next page. If there is more than one line on the first page of the speech, you simply write out on the next page the character's name again, and write "continued," in parentheses. This will look like JOHN *(continued)*.

- Generally, most playwrights use a 12-point font. Some playwrights like to use Courier New, but most use Times New Roman.

- All pages should be numbered. I like to place numbers at the bottom of the page in the center. The title page should not be numbered. If you must have a separate page for the time, place, and character information, make sure that that page is not numbered, either. With ten-minute play contests, if some play readers see a script that says 12 pages, they won't even open it to see that the title page and info page are part of that number. Begin your page numbers with the first page of dialogue

- If you are a Dramatists Guild member, you can include their logo on the title page on the bottom left-hand side.

TITLE OF YOUR PLAY

A Ten-Minute Play
By Your Name

Your address
Your city and state
Your e-mail address
Your phone number

Represented by:
Agent's Name
Name of Agency
Agency's address
Agency's city and state
Agent's e-mail address
Agent's phone number

© Year Your Name

(Copyright, which credits the playwright with legal ownership of his or her play, exists from the moment of the work's creation. The notice above may be used without registering your work with the U.S. Copyright Office; however, registration provides certain legal benefits; see www.copyright.gov.)

(Sample Format for Character, Time and Place Page
From my play *The Danger of Strangers*)

CAST OF CHARACTERS

HE—An attractive man in his thirties or early forties. Friendly and outgoing.

SHE—An attractive woman in her thirties or early forties. She is friendly and polite fully seductive.

TIME

The present, a hot August afternoon, lunchtime.

PLACE

The living room of a one-bedroom apartment in the West 50s overlooking Ninth Avenue in New York City. Bright sunlight is shining in from a window.

(An attractive man and woman are sitting opposite each other, just finishing their coffee. A small coffee table separates them. He's sweating but trying not to show it. She, on the other hand, doesn't seem to notice the heat at all.)

SHE: More?

HE: Hm?

SHE: Coffee.

HE: No, thanks.

SHE: Sure?

HE: Yeah?

SHE: You sure?

HE: Uh-huh.

A wink in his voice.

But I am tempted.

SHE: Are you?

HE: *You* are tempting me.

SHE: *(Slightly coy)* Am I?

HE: *(Leaning in a bit)* C'mon, you know you are.

SHE looks down at her coffee cup, lifts it to her lips, takes a sip. He watches her, then smiles.

SHE: What's so funny?

HE: Funny?

SHE: You're smiling.

HE: *(Playing with her)* Am I?

Chapter 6

Beginning Your Ten-Minute Play

Now that we've looked at a variety of ways to get started writing your ten-minute play, you may have some opening lines of dialogue, or a strong image. Or perhaps you're beginning from some sense of what you want your play to be about, or some idea of the characters you want to create. Or you may have created an outline for the play.

If you've working from an outline, don't feel that you must stick to it strictly as you progress with the play. Allow things to meander or evolve in any way they wish. If the characters go off in a different direction than you originally thought they would, go with them. Surprising yourself as you go along can be a thrilling creative experience. Outlines are starting points, road maps. But you can always take the road in another direction if you feel it would work better for your play.

About the only thing I'm thinking when I start out is that I'd like to write a ten-minute play. I may have a line of dialogue or a strong image or idea. But I have no idea what it will be about, or who the characters are. I'm open to anything and enjoy surprising myself. On some occasions, the play ends up turning into a one-act or a full-length. However it evolves, I let it write itself as much as I can, especially in the beginning.

How I Start My Ten-Minute Plays

As I mentioned, sometimes a line of dialogue is all I need to start a play. I may be on the subway, walking on the street, at the theater, etc., and I hear someone say something that I find interesting, a line that that somehow resonates with me. If I can, I'll jot it down for later. Something on the news can pique my interest. I hear someone say something about a situation they're involved with, and I connect to the words they use.

Or, sometimes, while I'm sitting at my computer a line will come to my mind out of nowhere. That line may end up opening the new play—or it may not. Sometimes it's just the trigger to get my imagination going.

Here are some examples of what I'm referring to from ten-minute plays I've written:

- "You're kidding, he said that?" This was the line that opened my ten-minute play *Coulda-Woulda-Shoulda*. The response to the line was "That's what he said, this morning when I was giving him his bath." From that first line and the response line, a play began for me about an overprotective mother and the problems this characteristic created between her and her husband. I allowed the opening dialogue to trigger my imagination and off I went, allowing the characters to just speak to each other.
- Another line that started one of my plays (*After*) was "My God, that was . . . !" The other character simply said, "What?" and then the first person said, "Eloquent!" For me that triggered something and the play began. The first speaker, a woman, is addressing a stranger she's just met at a funeral home, telling him how moved she was by his speech about the deceased. But I had no idea when I wrote that first exchange that I would use it in that way. In my imagination I wasn't sure where the conversation was taking place, and then somehow I pictured these two people standing in a funeral home, and that began the story of the play for me.
- In *Goin' Round on Rock Solid Ground*, the first line is "So?" And the other character says, "What?" The first character says "Tell me; tell me!" The second character then says, "Tell you what?!" The caginess of these two men gave me an idea about their relationship. I saw it taking place in a furnished basement—where I ultimately discovered that these two paranoid, lowlife guys were anxiously waiting a drug dealer.
- In *The Pain in the Poetry*, the line that kicked off the play was "I wrote a play." The other character, who is seated, looks up and says, "Hm, what?" The first character then says, "I said, I wrote a play!" The next character replies, "That's nice dear, did you feed the dog?" Something in that dialogue kicked in an image for me. I saw the second character sitting in a rocking chair, sewing. The play was

about a timid husband confessing to his controlling wife that he's secretively been writing a play for the last two years without her knowledge. Once again, I just let the characters continue speaking. I tried not to edit anything at this point. Whatever they wanted to say to each other was just fine with me.

What I'm trying to show with these examples is how I came to discover the thread for a play by simply starting with one line leading into another. Just as readers discover a book or play as they read it, I often discover my plays as I write them. It's very spontaneous. I enjoy not knowing where I'm going—until I do. There is the freedom that anything can happen and anything can be said at any moment. In fact, the dialogue that initially starts off a play may even be removed later on. Down the line you'll do rewrites, rewrites, rewrites. Sometimes the opening lines remain where they are; other times they are slightly altered or moved; and sometimes they are completely cut out. As I discover the play I'm writing I also discover what must be said—and when. Especially in the case of the ten-minute play, where every line should move the plot along, I try not to get too attached to any particular line or moment.

In all of the above examples I had no idea where I was going until the lines, the conversation, gave me a clue as to "who" was saying them. For example, what starts off as a man speaking can easily turn into a woman speaking as the characters begin to appear in my imagination.

Starting a Play with an Idea, a Theme, or an Image

Another way I start plays is when a particular issue comes to my mind and affects me in some way. I remember when I saw Tony Kushner's brilliant *Angels in America*. I left the theater high from the experience. Inspired by that brilliant play to write something about AIDS, I began two plays of my own the next morning. The first, *Unfamiliar Faces*, was about two gay men that realize that almost all their friends have died from the disease. It was a ten-minute play that went on to be an Actors Theatre of Louisville finalist.

I also started a second play, my first full-length, *Nobody's Flood*. It was a play about a family in the 1980s, dealing with the son's trying to hide the fact that he had AIDS. I've found that sometimes seeing other playwrights' work can be a great source of inspiration. For some writers, seeing a beautiful painting or sculpture, or being moved by some piece of music, is all they need to launch a new play.

The news can be another source of inspiration for me. I've started plays right after seeing a person on the news speaking about some horrible injustice or predicament. I've written plays on abortion, racial injustice, the economy, etc., based on some news story that moved me. Some of these plays have been ten-minute plays; others needed a larger canvas and became one-acts or even full-lengths. Whatever subject or idea moves you, touches you, makes you angry, or makes you laugh may be the seed for your play. If you need to, let the idea perk until you feel you need to express it. Don't be too concerned about the details of the characters at the beginning—whether they're male or female, their ages, or even what their names are—just write what they have to say. Quite often, I start a play with numbers rather than character names: "1" speaks to "2" or "3." I can always fill in the names when they come to me (generally through their dialogue). Whatever the issue is, allow the characters to discuss, argue, or lament about it as long as they need. Cutting will come later. At the beginning let them be affected by the struggle of the subject.

Go a museum or an art gallery. Allow other artists' paintings or sculptures to inspire you. Stephen Sondheim's brilliant musical *Sunday in the Park with George* was inspired by the painting *A Sunday Afternoon on the Island of La Grande Jatte* by George Seurat.

Personal issues, family conflicts, and unresolved real life incidents are quite often fodder for playwrights. The things we wanted to say, wish we had said, regret never saying, are often great starting points for plays. A great ten-minute play by Craig Lucas, called *What I Meant Was*, is one of my favorites. In this satiric play, members of a dysfunctional family say all the things they might have said if there was totally open communication. It's a raw, blisteringly funny play that shows what the truth looks like when there are no filters. It was a winner at the Actors Theatre of Louisville Humana Play Festival in the ten-minute play category and received a production there in 1996.

Probably some of the greatest advice I ever received about playwriting is "Write what you're afraid to write about." Once you open that door, it's amazing what can come out of you. Yes, it requires a certain amount of bravery, but believe me, the payoff for both you and your audience will be well worth it.

Chapter 7

The Next Steps

Intention, Objective, and Action

Once I start to get some sense of who my characters are, I also begin to get a sense of *what they want*. This is one of the most important moments of discovering what my play is actually about. Ask yourself early on in the writing of your play "What do my lead characters want?"

Actors are taught in acting classes that they must always know what their character wants (the *objective*). They are told to make it personal (the *intention*) and then go for it (the *action*). As writers, we have to supply actors with characters that have strong wants, or they won't have much to play. Simply put, the stronger the wants, the more the actor has to play.

To illustrate this important point: my objective now is to teach you, the reader, how to write a ten-minute play. I'm sitting at my computer trying to figure out the best ways I can communicate the meaning of this particular terminology to you. I am determined to find the right words (intention), and by choosing and writing these words that you're now reading, I hope to get this important aspect of writing a ten-minute play through to you (action).

When working on a ten-minute play you have to be certain that your main character has a strong need. All the other characters (and hopefully there aren't too many others in your ten-minute play), should also have needs that they may or (may not) fulfill. Because this is a ten-minute play, you want to make these character intentions obvious in (hopefully) the first two pages of your play. This is no time to mess around with a lot of exposition. Get to the point ASAP! Sometimes this means that you over-write during your first draft. Write as much as you need to set the story in motion.

When it's all there, no matter how many pages you have, then cut, cut, cut down to the bone, to the basics of the story you need to tell in ten pages. This is where the play actually begins. The trick is to cut just the fat from your storytelling, not the muscle. You must have a cohesive, strong, clear story from the get-go, with characters motivated by strong needs. As your characters interact, trying to have their needs met, you create the universe of your play and the story reveals itself.

The Setting and Time

Where you set the play will definitely influence the story you're telling. If you set the play in a prison cell, your characters are going to have very different realities than they would if you placed them at a kitchen table.

The time of day, whether it's two in the morning or two in the afternoon, will affect the characters' behavior. There are different rhythms for different times of day or night.

Setting your play on a sweltering hot summer night, or a freezing cold day with little or no heat, will also affect how characters behave.

The Best Way to Tell Your Story: The Play's Structure

Plays take several forms. They can be naturalistic and have a traditional structure (beginning, middle, and end) or they can tell a story in a nontraditional or nonlinear way. The story of your play and the characters' interactions can guide you as to which form fits best. Initially you may want to allow your play to move in any direction (and form) that it wants. As it becomes clearer to you, you'll have a better idea of how you want to tell the story. I have written plays that started off with a traditional structure and eventually called for a major rewrite, switching to a nonlinear structure. With a ten-minute play this isn't too difficult an adjustment. Just make sure the structure of the completed draft is consistent so that your story comes through clearly.

Complications Arise

The story line in a ten-minute play should be more complicated than just the interaction of characters with strong needs. On the other hand, you don't want to create complications in your story that are not resolvable in ten pages. Perhaps a minor character needs conflict with your lead character to increase the drama. Or perhaps you can introduce an event that will alter the path of the story that you've started with. The last thing you want is a play that is predictable, where the audience is ahead of you because your conclusion is so obvious. Of course, the event must be believable and make sense with the facts of your story up to that point. I have seen many short plays in which the playwright seemed to have thrown something in just for "effect," and it didn't seem truthful to the story as a whole.

Realizing and Developing the Story of the Play

For me, there is usually an aha point somewhere along the line, where I "really get" what my play is about. I realize what story I'm trying to tell and who these characters are. Following that realization, I start working to make the story clearer. I've come to know who my main character is and what exactly he or she wants. Generally the other character(s) in the play have to be part of the conflict that the lead character is trying to overcome. (When, say, the two characters in the play are both trying to overcome a major threat to earth, or a plague, or some scenario like that, the obstacle is the unseen.) In either case, I need to know what specifically is in the way of the protagonist getting what he or she wants (the obstacle). These elements are the foundation for the first draft of that ten-minute play.

Sometimes the more I plunge into the play, the more I become an active participant. I feel the feelings of the characters as they discover their challenges and try to overcome them. I identify with their conflict and feel their frustrations as they attempt to overcome them.

Perhaps it's the actor in me, but I generally speak the dialogue as I write it, or right after I write it. I'm not sure if other playwrights do that. I know some writers can sit in a coffee shop and silently write their plays. I need to say the lines out loud, see how they feel. Sometimes I need to get up, move around, take the action that's called for.

As I begin to speak and embody the words I write, the play takes off, and a very rough first draft starts to emerge. I'm still trying to get my characters fleshed out, see what their conflicts are, and figure out how they may resolve them. I constantly return to the opening dialogue and follow the trail of the play I've written so far. My mind becomes a bit more analytical as I make small "refinements" along the way; a word here or a line there. Anything that, in the moment, feels right. Sometimes it becomes apparent that some dialogue needs to be placed earlier or later in the play, or maybe even removed as it no longer is necessary to tell the story. Reading through the play also helps me to ensure that all of the characters are necessary, and that all of them have a definite throughline.

You must always keep in mind that what you're writing is a ten-minute play, so everything must move the story forward. There is no line or moment or action that should digress for long enough to throw the story off track in even the slightest way. Once again, it's not only what must be said, but what must be said now! That said, don't confuse digression with a real change of direction. When the audience is ahead of you and can predict the outcome, you've lost their interest. Surprise yourself as you go along and you'll surprise them.

As you keep rereading what you've written and fine-tuning your work, you should see your creation emerge from an amorphous state into a defined, specific play.

Actors Working on Their Plays

Actors, since perhaps up until now you've only acted in plays, take this opportunity to act in your *own* play. While writing it, read it aloud. As you're reading, do your characters feel real to you? Do you understand what their intentions are? Can you feel the dynamic between your lead character and the other characters in your play? Start off reading only the words you've written so far, but then allow yourself (perhaps with some improvisation) to open up the dialogue where it feels necessary. Eliminate lines of dialogue that don't feel real. Feel free to immerse yourself as an actor in your play, playing all the roles. If you like, get up, move around as the characters; see how that feels. Stay concentrated, in the moment, and you'll see where things do and don't work. Here's where the actor in you starts to become the critic of your own play. Trust your actor's instincts to guide you as you observe what's working and what isn't.

See if you can feel the play moving towards its conclusion. If not, try to see where it veers off course.

Ending the First Draft

To me, the most important moments of my plays are the opening and closing moments. I feel that the opening moments give the audience a peek into a whole new world. The closing moment is like saying good-bye to that world. The ending of your play must always be earned by the story that precedes it. Playwriting is storytelling. It's as simple as "Once upon a time . . . " After you've opened the box, the story unfolds.

Finding Your Title

The title is the first thing readers discover about your play. It can be a metaphor about your play or something descriptive. Descriptive titles don't always resonate well and may even be somewhat boring. I personally prefer metaphoric titles. Metaphoric titles at their best hint at the theme of the play and can be very enticing to a reader. A metaphoric title can have a double meaning, which is especially effective after a reader has read your play and then reflects on it.

Your play's title may come from a line of dialogue, or a character's name, or from what you feel the play is about. It can come to you in a flash, or after some reflection on the theme of your play. It may come to you after you've finished writing the first or second draft. There's nothing wrong with changing titles as many times as you wish (before you send out the finished play). Most importantly, the title should communicate in just a few words some essence of what you feel your play is trying to say.

After the First Draft

The first draft of your play really is about *discovery*: discovering what the play is about, the story you're trying to tell. It may well run over ten pages as you allow the story room to unfold.

Once I've completed the first draft I sometimes put it away. I want to come back to it fresh before I start any major rewrites. You may discover on a later read that ideas, moments, that you thought there were there, actually aren't there. What you thought was on the page may be still in your mind. Now you have another opportunity to make sure it's on the page.

Sometimes I find myself thinking about the play even when I'm not consciously working on it. I try to clear my mind and go on to other things. But then perhaps while I'm on the treadmill, having dinner, or even just out walking, a light will go on about some aspect of the play. Sometimes it's a word, or a line of dialogue, or it may be a plot point that I hadn't thought about. Or I'll have some epiphany that will shed light on what the play is

really about. It might mean that when I go back to working on the play I'll
have to change major plot points, or eliminate an unnecessary character, or
any one of a million other things. If the thought seems important enough,
I might jot it down. Or, I might let it ferment in my mind until I actually
get back to work on the play at my computer.

Neil Simon, in his book *Rewrites: A Memoir*, discusses coming back
to a play after he's put it away for a while. He says, "When I take it out and
reread it . . . what's good remains good, but what's bad jumps off the page
and smacks me right across my ego."

Chapter 8

Reading the First Draft

After you've completed the first draft of your ten-minute play, check the following list and see if it helps you in tightening your script. You should refer to this guideline periodically, using it for subsequent revisions.

Sometimes it helps to try to read the script anew, as if you hadn't written it. I know that seems a bit odd, but you can pretend you haven't read it before.

1. From the very first line, does the script engage you? The moment you feel disengaged, just mark the passage(s), then continue reading. Don't analyze or try to fix anything at this point.
2. Wherever you feel the play loses you (becomes too convoluted, confusing), mark the section.
3. Do you believe the characters? Do they seem fully realized? If not, at which point do you feel they lose you? Be as specific as you can; underline the line or moment.
4. Does the way each character speaks sound authentic? Mark the words or passages that sound false.
5. Are there any characters that seem too similar to other characters?
6. Do you care about these characters? Do they offend you, annoy you, seem too abrasive?
7. Are all of your characters in this draft necessary? Can any of them be combined, eliminated?
8. Do you feel at any point that there's too much narrative or exposition? Remember, with a ten-minute play too much exposition is a waste of space.
9. Do you notice any repetition in the dialogue, the same words or phrases being overused?

10. Do you feel that there is a repetition in the ideas being expressed? Are some characters expressing the same ideas repeatedly?
11. Is it clear what you're trying to say in this play?
12. Is the theme of the play clear?
13. Does the ending make sense? Is it logical; was it earned?
14. How do you feel after finishing the piece? Do you feel satisfied that you accomplished what you set out to do?
15. Do you wish there was more? Do you feel that there was too much of any one element, character, scene, etc?
16. Are you happy with the title of your play? Does it work for the play that you've written?

At What Point Should You Have Someone Else Read What You've Written?

Some playwrights skip this step and go right to having readings of their play. It's up to you. Having someone read your play and give you feedback can be helpful—or not. It depends on you and the person you've given the script to.

Some writers want to get feedback on their first draft as soon as they've finished working on it. Getting it to someone you trust for a response at the right time can be very helpful. But getting it to a reader prematurely is not a good idea. Before you give your play to someone, make sure that you genuinely feel that there is nothing at this time that you can do to improve it.

Once you let others comment on your work, they become a part of your relationship with your material. Their input, comments, and suggestions may have an impact on your rewrites. You may even want to wait until the second draft before handing your work over to someone else. There is no rule on this; only you will know when the time is right.

Selecting the Right Person to Read Your First Draft

Whom you ask to read your manuscript is very important. You should trust and respect the opinion of the person that you're asking to read your material. You should feel that your reader can comment intelligently and supportively, and help with any problems they see in your text. Remember, no matter whom you choose, he or she is just one person, with an individual and subjective point of view. At the end of the day, it's always your opinion that carries the most weight; it's your baby.

Do not expect or allow the reader that you've selected to give you solutions to problems or suggestions as to how you should rewrite your play. You are not collaborating. The best readers are the ones that can pose the right questions to you, not give you answers.

The First Reading of Your Play

At some point after you've completed the first draft of your play, you should have a reading to hear what you have. You can have a private reading of your play at your home or a public one in a writers' or actors' group. Readings of first drafts of a play can be tricky in several ways. I've learned that sometimes very talented actors can make a play with problems seem like it doesn't have them. These actors have the ability to "fill in" moments that really aren't in the dialogue. On the other side of the coin, less experienced or talented actors can sometimes make a good script sound like it's not quite there yet. It's for that reason that I generally have at least two or even three readings of my new plays with different groups, and with different actors. If I'm seeing the same problems occurring in the script at each reading, then I know it's something that needs to be addressed.

Cold Readings of Your Ten-Minute Play

I personally don't like to have cold readings of my plays. I know that many actor-playwright groups meet and hand out scripts to actors to read, absolutely cold. The problem I have with this is that, since the actors haven't actually read the script previously, they may go off in a wrong direction. Many good actors are simply not the best cold readers. And with experimental, absurd, poetic, or nontraditional plays, actors and audiences can easily become confused during a first reading and go off course.

I try to get actors my scripts a day or so in advance so that they can prepare. This doesn't always work out, but for me it's the best scenario. If I have a chance to discuss the piece with them in advance, that's even better. That way we all know we're on the same page. With a ten-minute play, actors don't need too much time to absorb the material, but I like them to be familiar with the material before the reading.

Should You Be an Actor in the First Readings of Your Ten-Minute Play?

No. For you to be able to really hear the initial readings of your play and do any necessary rewrites, you must be able to stand back and hear your play objectively—along with any comments that the first listeners make. It's best during these initial readings to sit in the rear of the group, where you can not only hear your play but also watch the audience. Notice any body language that may indicate that they're not into it. Since it is only a ten-minute play, most people shouldn't get restless or move around too much unless there is something wrong with the play and/or reading.

Listening to Feedback and Comments

Learning how to find value in comments can help you in your rewrites. So can knowing how to deal with negative or unhelpful comments. Opinions are like noses; everyone's got one. Try to be as neutral as possible and take the comments about your play with some detachment. I know that this is difficult because this is your baby, and you may feel very vulnerable as others comment on it (sometimes harshly), but the more you can just hear their comments without feeling like your play or your talent is being attacked, the better the reading will serve you.

Do not dispute the comments that are made about your play; just take them in. Don't justify anything that you feel was criticized. Praise should be accepted with appreciation but not given any more weight than the negative, harsher comments. It's always nice to know someone "got" your play and what you were trying to do. But whether a comment is positive or negative, it's likely to be subjective. We all have our own history, which can color our opinions. Try to ascertain where the commenter is coming from. This isn't always easy when folks are tearing your play apart.

Not Allowing Others to Rewrite Your Play

I see this a lot at play readings. People, trying to help, will make suggestions about how to fix this or that moment, or how to end your play, or how to make a character more sympathetic, believable, etc. Hopefully, the narrator who is running the group will ask them to refrain from those sorts of suggestions.

If someone has a comment that totally baffles you, feel free to ask him or her to rephrase the question. If you still don't understand, ask him or her to please be more specific and if possible to refer to the section of the play that inspired the comment. At what particular moment of your play did the person become lost during the reading? What things didn't make sense or seemed illogical? The more specific the speaker can be, the more helpful their comments will be to you.

If everyone in the group makes the same comment about some aspect of your play, you may want to take a look at what they're saying. If you still feel you don't agree with them, don't change it. Try having the play read in another group. See if that point comes up again. If it does, then take another look at the point both groups have made.

There are sometimes group politics involved when people comment on plays. For instance, comments may reflect the general esteem in which some playwrights are held rather than the merits or flaws of a particular piece.

Some people making comments just like to hear themselves talk and to show everyone how intelligent they are. Take that into consideration when listening.

Again, just listen and take everything in, good and bad. In the end only you will know what actually needs to be addressed.

Back to Rewrites

Sometimes I take a break from working on the play and return to it at a later time. But if I received comments during the reading(s) that clicked for me, or I'm really hot on that particular play and genuinely feel I might be able to fix the problem, I continue on to the rewriting phase of the play, with these points in mind:

- Is this the story you wanted to tell?
- Is the conflict clearer?
- Are the characters better defined?
- Is there a clearer beginning, middle, and end?
- Does the play have a clear arc?
- Were you able to infuse any comments from the readings that you felt were appropriate into this draft?

- Are you satisfied with this new draft? Not just satisfied to the point that you feel "things can be worked out in production." If it's not on the page it's not on the stage. You can't expect directors and actors to make a play work that you honestly feel is not ready when you hand it out.
- Is this the play you meant to write?

Chapter 9

Getting Your Play Out

Your ten-minute play only has value when you send it out into the world.
I have known playwrights that complete their hard work on their play
and then, perhaps because of fear of rejection, put it away in their drawer,
sometimes for years. Your play needs to be read. More importantly, your
play needs to be produced, performed. You can only do so many rewrites.
You can only do so many readings. You can only so many workshops.
Eventually the play needs to be submitted to theaters doing ten-minute play
festivals and to ten-minute play competitions.

There are several resources you can use to help determine where to
send your ten-minute play. The Theater Communications Group's *Dramatists Sourcebook* and the *Dramatists Guild Resource Directory* are two
dependable sources. I also have had a great deal of luck with Google. Punch
in searches for ten-minute plays, ten-minute play festivals, ten-minute
playwriting competitions, and publishers of ten-minute plays. Also, don't
limit your choices only to the U.S. You'd be surprise how many possibilities
are out there all over the world, and many accept American plays.

Read the listing information carefully. If they say they only accept plays
until November, don't bother sending yours in December. You missed their
cutoff point. Some theaters charge a small reader's fee. Fortunately, this is
becoming less and less common. I personally don't support theaters that do
this and generally won't send my plays to them. I don't believe playwrights
submitting their work should be charged a fee to have it read. This is an
expense I feel the theaters should absorb in their budgets.

You should become familiar with the type of plays a theater produces
before you send in your play. Check out their Web site. If it's a small community theater that plays to mostly a family audience, your very R-rated,
adult play is not a good fit. If they are only looking for plays about people
of color, or plays by or about women, and that doesn't pertain to you, don't

send your play to them. They'll resent that you've wasted their time and resources. Community theaters, church theaters, and high school theater companies generally want plays that are family friendly. Other theaters are looking for edgy, adult plays. Determine where your play fits best. You're not going to change their sensibilities about their theater, even if your play is terrific.

If a theater says they don't accept unsolicited scripts, don't send yours. If they say they only accept one submission per playwright, don't send two. If they charge a submission fee, make sure a check for the correct amount is made out with the correct name of the payee. When they say they only want plays that have not had a professional production and you've had several, don't send it and hope they won't find out.

All submissions for your ten-minute play (or any play, for that matter) should always include the play, your letter of introduction, a synopsis of the play, and your resume (if requested).

Many playwrights seem to have trouble writing a letter of introduction. Basically what you're doing here is telling them why you feel this particular ten-minute play is a good fit for their theater. You don't need to give a hard sell about how great the play is and how everyone who's ever heard it read has loved it. You should keep the letter of introduction short and to the point. When it comes to discussing your play you certainly want to make it appealing to them, but be careful not to try to oversell. I've read many letters of introductions by playwrights; some sound coldly business-like, and others are way too chummy. Try to find the middle ground: warm, but professional. Mostly you want to make them want to read your play.

As for the ten-minute play you're sending, make sure it's securely bound. You can find very inexpensive folders at many business outlets online, or you can staple it.

You don't want to send the play out until you're certain it's ready. Once it's sent to theaters and contests, that's it. Should you decide to do further rewrites on the play, you shouldn't send them the updated version unless they contact you about their interest in producing the version that you originally sent. If they do contact you and tell you they're interested in your play or have chosen your play, you can mention it then, if you feel it's advisable. If they've contacted you, they obviously like the play you sent them. If your rewrite isn't too extensive, perhaps a nip or tuck here or there, you may choose to tell them. If however, you've done a major rewrite (i.e., plot or character changes, etc.) you might be best advised not to offer it to them. Bottom line, it's your play, and you can do what you feel is best for your play. Just be aware of the consequences with either of these decisions.

You don't need to buy expensive envelopes to mail your play out. Simple manila envelopes that you can buy by the box at a Staples or Office Depot should be fine. If you're looking to cut costs, two writing magazines, *The Writers Digest* and *The Writer*, advertise discount office supplies.

Only some of the theaters that produce ten-minute plays recommend that you include an envelope with postage (SASE) for them to return your play when they're finished with it. When submitting your play, see what that particular theater recommends.

Some playwrights like to include a self-addressed, stamped postcard (SASP) with their submissions as an easy way for theaters to confirm receipt of the play. Some theaters may even include a note on the returned postcard letting entrants know when they'll be making their final decisions.

E-mail Submissions

Always include a message with e-mailed submissions, and make that message short and to the point. There is no need to go into the history of the play. If the theater has requested any information about previous productions and/or any publication of the play, make sure you include it. Many theaters and festivals will not produce your play in their festival if it's been published or has had a major production. Readings, workshops, and staged readings, however, are unlikely to disqualify a submission. Always check with the theater beforehand. As in a cover letter, you want to pique their interest in your play without too hard a sell.

Actors: Should You Be in the First Production of Your Play?

I advise against it if at all possible. As with the initial readings, you want to see how your play plays and how an audience responds to it in a professional production. I realize that you may have written the play originally as a vehicle for yourself, but *if you can*, hold off until future productions. You may identify changes you want to make even at this stage, for future productions—and hopefully your ten-minute play will have many productions.

I realize that some of you, no matter what, want to be in the first production of your play. If you must, realize that you will be wearing two hats, writer and actor. Your relationship with the director also may be challenging when you are the actor in your own play. You don't want to usurp their power or decisions because "you know better."   You should try to be diplomatic when having talks with the director (privately) about the play. Know which hat you're wearing and try to be objective and not get emotionally involved during the discussions. Since it's your play, the other actors may look to you for advice, insights, or direction, especially on how you see their character. Stay clear of any giving any feedback or allowing them to come to you for help. Your only role should be that of another actor in the production. Simply refer them to your director. Set these ground rules with your cast early on, at the first rehearsal.

Chapter 10

Interviews with Playwrights of Ten-Minute Plays

What follows are interviews with some well-respected playwrights who have had a fair amount of success with their ten-minute plays. I specifically asked questions that I felt would be of value to playwrights as well as actor/playwrights. I found many of the responses to the interview questions insightful and illuminating. When different playwrights answer the same question in similar terms, it's a probably a sign that the advice may be of value. You'll also notice that several of the playwrights have a difference of opinion on certain matters pertaining to ten-minute plays. See which advice is most helpful to you while working on your play. I've tried to include playwrights from different backgrounds, countries, and approaches.

Jenny Lyn Bader

Jenny Lyn Bader has published seven ten-minute plays in Smith & Kraus's annual *Best Ten-Minute Play* series: *The Popcorn Sonata* (City Theatre); *Past Lives* (Center Stage, NY); *The Third First Blind Double Date* (New Georges Performathon); *One Night at Your Local Superstore* (Café Theatre at George St. Playhouse), *Valentine's Play* (Stageworks/ Hudson), *Best Friends* (W.E.T./"The Love Plays"), and *Oppression and Pearls* (Largo at the Coronet Theatre, Los Angeles/"Standing on Ceremony"). Other short works include *Worldness* (Humana Festival of New American Plays, Actors Theatre of Louisville), published by Dramatists Play Service in *Heaven and Hell*; *Miss America* (New York International Fringe Festival, "Best of the Fringe" selection); and

The Joint Collection (Mile Square Productions). Her full-length plays include *Mona Lisa Speaks* (Core Ensemble); *In Flight,* which won the North American Actors Association Playreading Festival in London; *Manhattan Casanova,* winner of the Edith Oliver Award (Eugene O'Neill Theater Center); and *None of the Above* (New Georges), available from Dramatists Play Service. She is director of artistic development at Theatre 167.

Glenn Alterman: What was it like for you writing your first ten-minute play? Was it your plan to write a ten-minute play, or did it just work out that way?

Jenny Lyn Bader: I immediately enjoyed the experience of having to set up a play so quickly. I love writing beginnings, and the beginnings of short plays can fly particularly fast.

There was a point in time when a lot of theaters began doing ten-minute plays instead of short works of more varied lengths. One reason for that trend was the popularity of the Actors Theatre of Louisville's National Ten-Minute Play Contest, a well-respected institution that has launched a few careers. Perhaps another reason was the "squishability" factor. Theaters found they could squish more plays into a single evening, establishing relationships with more writers. I believe the first one I ever wrote was written for such an evening. The theater announced a theme and invited a bunch of writers to submit. So the first time I wrote one I did know it was supposed to be ten minutes long.

But it's certainly happened that I've written a ten-minute play when I wasn't meaning to do so. One of my first ten-minute plays I had planned as a full-length. . . . There was a commissioning program at a regional theater, and I applied to it with a script outline and proposal for a full-length play called *The Third First Blind Double Date.* The literary manager wrote me a nice note saying that the commissioning program had unexpectedly lost its funding and they wouldn't be paying anyone to write any plays, but their script committee had been intrigued by my idea. They thought it was a wonderful idea for a play and said they thought I should go ahead and write it anyway.

This glimmer of encouragement was invaluable to me at that early point in my career when most people just look at you funny if you say you have an idea for a play. So I sat down to write the full play. The idea seemed like a complex theatrical one, offbeat and somewhat experimental, and I imagined it would take much time and space to execute. But suddenly I found the whole idea coming out at once: quickly, concisely, and in ten pages.

At first I was concerned that the play wanted to be shorter than I wanted it to be. But plays do want things, and I think it's best to listen to them.

The opposite has happened, too. I once started writing what I intended to be a ten-minute play and the characters simply wouldn't stop talking to each other—and that became a full-length play. The play wants what it wants. And characters often have minds of their own, too.

Alterman: Did you come up against any obstacles in writing your first ten-minute play? If so, what were they and how did you overcome them?

Bader: The main obstacle is always figuring out how to put a whole play in a space that would normally be reserved for a scene or two—and taking its structure seriously. Naturally I had the usual "second act problems—what in the film business would be called "third act problems," and what in the ten-minute play business might more accurately be called "page nine problems." You don't want the energy to sag as you are nearing the end of your story. So around page nine, I had to figure out what might be exciting enough to top what had come before.

In one case, the play, *Myth America, You Are Beautiful*, written for the Primary Stages American Myths Project and later expanded into *Miss America*, involved two pageant contestants: a traditional beauty queen and a contemporary, politically correct contestant. In private, the politically correct contestant, Miss California, who is the more smooth and polished of the two, gives the politically incorrect one, Miss Texas, her careerist vision of the pageant. I wanted her words to come back later to jeopardize her chance at the crown. I thought Miss Texas might simply repeat what Miss California had said privately in public. But on page nine, I said that there's no way out . . . until I think of something better. Then I decided that it should come out that Miss Texas, a scrappy, self-made gal not above a few underhanded tricks, was taping their conversation—so when we hear Miss California's words again, we hear her own voice on a recording, in a dramatic moment where Miss Texas makes a plea for the crown and also reveals she has been wearing a wire.

In this particular case, I took a potentially dull event—one character repeats what another has said—and made it into a more dramatic one. I did so by making the event more physical and more theatrical. It also added a layer of intrigue, providing more of a payoff of the scene that had come before. In every ten-minute play I write, I try to push myself to offer an unexpected twist before the play ends, whether it's a story twist or an emotional twist.

Alterman: Do you find working on ten-minute plays any different from working on one-acts or full-lengths? If so, how?

Bader: Ten-minute plays are written with greater economy and efficiency. In a way, it's a little like writing a poem. In another way, it's a lot like writing a play that's been condensed. The challenge is to compress the dramatic experience. How can a play that clocks in at ten minutes have the excitement, the impact, the emotion of a full-length play? I feel that the structure needs to be managed a little differently, too. Unlike a full-length, where setups and payoffs are layered in over time, a ten-minute play has a setup that gets paid off momentarily. So you need to be careful that this doesn't feel too clunky—that payoff doesn't follow setup one page later. In a way sometimes the setup has to be more subtle. If you're trying to set up a mystery or a question in a full-length, the audience has 50 pages or more to forget about it. But anything you plant in a ten-minute play they may remember all too well. That makes it important for you to avoid obvious setups. But it also gives you the chance to offer a lot more payoffs. You can pay off several different setups and feel pretty confident that the audience will recall them all, since they just saw them planted a few minutes ago.

Alterman: What do you feel constitutes a good ten-minute play?

Bader: The best ones hit all the marks of a full-length play. There should be a beginning, middle, and end. It should have story surprises, like an ending that seems to go one way and goes another. It should move at a clip, with pacing that is strong throughout and accelerates toward the end. It should have a structure, not just a texture. Each character should have a journey or character arc—growing or causing another character to develop.

The very best ones tell a story in a unique voice, offer up a complete world, and somehow defy expectations.

Alterman: What mistakes have you noticed writers make when working on ten-minute plays?

Bader: I've seen writers who feel an interesting conversation, perhaps one that they had or overheard, makes a fine ten-minute play. Or that an intriguing mood is enough to sustain a play that's so brief. Or that they can just ruminate on an idea or image for ten minutes. But even the shortest play has to get you from point A to point B. The biggest mistake writers make is staying on point A, repeating an idea without development, or writing a one-joke comedy, where characters reiterate their point of view and gain no insights. A novice playwright will think that just because a play is very short it must be more like writing a scene or a sketch. But a scene and a sketch do not need to accomplish as much as a play, do not need to have as much of a sense of movement and transformation.

Alterman: Do you have any additional advice for writers who are about to attempt their first ten-minute play?

Bader:

- Try to draft as much of it as you can in one sitting, which can help give the piece a sense of momentum. If you can't finish and need to set it aside, at least make notes or an outline for the rest of the play.
- When you return to the draft, ask how you can give it more clarity and shape.
- Be a ruthless editor—every line should have a purpose.
- Maximize the sense of conflict in the time and space provided.
- Consider the theme that you are expressing, think of how you might deepen the expression of that theme, and make sure its counter-argument is also expressed.
- Try reading it aloud, not just as a whole, but once through from the point of view of each character to make sure each character has a through line and moments of discovery—and, where possible, that each actor has a variety of emotional opportunities. Imagine from the perspective of each character how you might make that person more defined, more layered, and more complex.
- Ask yourself where the climax of the play is and if tension is building up toward that point.
- If you want it to be widely produced, use only one set. Many theaters will not produce short plays that require set changes.
- Surprise yourself by creating an unexpected moment.
- Always remember: it's not a ten-minute scene, it's a ten-minute play.

Don Nigro

Don Nigro is the author of over 300 plays, and his work is produced all over the world. Samuel French has published 135 of his plays in acting editions. Many times a finalist for Actors Theatre of Louisville's Heideman Award, he has written multiple works featured in Lawrence Harbison's yearly *Best Ten-Minute Plays* and other anthologies.

Glenn Alterman: What was it like for you writing your first ten-minute play? Was it your plan to write a ten-minute play, or did it just work out that way?

Don Nigro: I am by nature an irrational, instinctive sort of playwright. I don't trust rules, don't believe in rules, don't want anybody telling me there are rules. My approach is to trust the impulse, however strange, and see what happens. This has resulted in plays of all shapes and sizes, investigating a great many different sorts of conventions, often subverting, blending, maybe inventing them. So I probably happened to write a number of ten-minute plays without thinking of them as that. They were just shorter plays where the impulse resulted in something that happened to play ten minutes or less. It was Actors Theatre of Louisville that actually got me paying attention to staying at or under the ten-minute playing time, through their contest, and for a number of years I found that sooner or later in any given year I would come up with something that met their criteria, and to my surprise I actually enjoyed that. I never forced anything to be a ten-minute play. I just observed when something I was writing had the potential to be that, and if it turned out to be one, I sent it to them.

Alterman: Did you come up against any obstacles in writing your first ten-minute play? If so, what were they and how did you overcome them?

Nigro: Sometimes a play will start out fine and just stop on you. Or you'll seem to have finished it but you can't help feeling there's something missing or something wrong with it, but you're not sure what it is; or you think you know what's wrong but don't know how to fix it at the moment. I keep pushing at it, but if it continues to resist, I never force it. I'll put it away for a while. Now and then I would write something that I thought was going to be a ten-minute play, but it just wanted to be a little longer. Not much longer, just a few minutes. But if it really felt to me like that's what it needed to be, I never cut things out just to pare it down for the sake of some contest or something. If the play wants to be a twelve-minute play, let it be a twelve-minute play, and send it somewhere else. I did cut *The Sin Eater* a bit when Louisville wanted to produce it, because it was running long and it was in a program with other playwrights who were all operating under the same restrictions, but I restored the cuts in the printed version, so it actually plays several minutes longer now. What I cut was several things the director really liked, but things not absolutely essential to the structure. It's a better play with those things restored, but it's no longer a ten-minute play.

Alterman: Do you find working on ten-minute plays any different from working on one-acts or full-lengths? If so, how?

Nigro: In some respects, with a shorter play, you have more freedom to be a little crazier, to try odd things that perhaps you couldn't sustain for a longer period of time. In the theater you are always limited by the amount of time you can actually get people to sit and pay attention. They are more likely to put up with something bizarre for fifteen minutes than for two hours. But when you get down to ten minutes, there's another sense in which you have less freedom, because every second matters. Of course, that's also true for *Long Day's Journey Into Night* or any play, regardless of the length—every second of every play matters, and you don't want more than you need, ever, whether the play lasts three hours or five minutes. It's just that in a ten-minute play, you have fewer seconds. Everything counts. Again, true for any play, but you can kid yourself with a longer one, maybe. In a ten-minute universe, you can't kid yourself. Either a moment helps you get where you're going or it doesn't. If it doesn't, that's what you cut. The ten-minute form makes this very clear to you as you're working.

Alterman: What do you feel constitutes a good ten-minute play?

Nigro: I suppose what constitutes a good ten-minute play is what constitutes any good play, of whatever length: it pulls you in and gets you to care and carries you along to a place you didn't realize you were going that, once you get there, feels mysteriously inevitable. You've just got less time to do this in a ten-minute play. Not easy. But it can be very satisfying. A full-length play like *King Lear* is the dovetailing of many smaller actions into one larger one, like streams flowing into a river. A ten-minute play tends to manifest one swift, clean action. But if it's a good one, it suggests a whole complex universe of possible implications.

Alterman: What mistakes have you noticed writers make when working on ten-minute plays?

Nigro: I don't want to characterize other people's work, but mistakes I'd try to avoid would be trying to stuff too much into the box, or presuming that because it's so short, structure doesn't matter, or, conversely, presuming that because it's so short, structure is the only thing that matters. Sometimes a two-minute song can be a more powerful experience than a grand opera. But it's got to be done just right. And that, for me, is mostly a matter of instinct. You hope you start out with good instincts, and that your instincts get better as you learn more. But you've got to trust them. If the play feels right to me, then I just trust it. What looks like a mistake to you might be the best part to somebody else.

Alterman: Do you have any additional advice for writers who are about to attempt their first ten-minute play?

Nigro: Don't force it to be one if it doesn't want to be. Let it be what it is. You can always write another play.

Craig Pospisil

Craig Pospisil is the author of *Months on End*, *Somewhere In Between*, *The Dunes*, *Life Is Short*, and the collection *Choosing Sides*, all published by Dramatists Play Service. He has written over 50 ten-minute plays, including 16 short plays and musicals written for theAtrainplays. His "A train plays" include *It's Not You*, *Tourist Attraction*, and *The Best Way to Go*, which are published by Playscripts in Volumes 1 and 2 of *theAtrainplays*. *It's Not You* has been produced over 100 times around the country and the world, translated into Chinese, published in *An Anthology of Contemporary American Short Plays in Beijing*, and is also part of the collection *Take Ten II: New Ten-Minute Plays*. *Tourist Attraction* is collected in *Best Stage Scenes 2006*. Other short plays include *On the Edge in Under Thirty: Plays for a New Generation*, and *Best Ten-Minute Plays 2005*; *Perchance the Best Ten-minute Plays 2006* and *There's No Here Here*, which will appear in *Best Ten-Minute Plays 2012*. He is a six-time finalist for the Heideman Award, and won the Alan Minieri Memorial Playwriting Award for *The American Dream Revisited*. For more information: www.CraigPospisil.com.

Glenn Alterman: What was it like for you writing your first ten-minute play? Was it your plan to write a ten-minute play, or did it just work out that way?

Craig Pospisil: I didn't set out to write a ten-minute play the first time I wrote one. The first one really came about because I was taking a scene writing class the summer before deciding to go to graduate school. The first couple of pieces I wrote were scenes that were imagined to be from a longer play, which didn't exist. I didn't find that very satisfying, because they felt incomplete to me. So for the other assignments I just started writing full stories—short plays with their own beginning, middle, and end—and I discovered I really liked the form. Something about the compact nature of them appealed to me, and I kept having ideas for new ones. I submitted several of the short plays from that class along with a full-length play of mine when I applied to the Dramatic Writing Program at New York University, where I ended up going. Eventually a couple of those first ten-minute plays wound up inspiring me and becoming part of a full-length play of mine called *Somewhere In Between*.

Alterman: Did you come up against any obstacles in writing your first ten-minute play? If so, what were they and how did you overcome them?

Pospisil: Strangely, I think one of the obstacles of a ten-minute play is keeping the stakes for the characters high. Because these plays are so short, there's a temptation to set up whatever the problem is for the characters and then leave it at that, have the characters argue back and forth at the same level for the whole script. That can get deadly even in a short play, and ten minutes can seem a lot longer than you'd think. Because of the time limit you really need to keep increasing the stakes, increasing the pressure on your characters all the time. By doing that you not only keep the story moving and active, but you make the characters richer and more interesting to the audience.

I have a short play called *Guerilla Gorilla* that's set in a future where the theater has been made illegal. A young man and woman are trying to get tickets to an underground production of a play. She's really fired up to see it, and he's scared they'll be arrested, but he's very attracted to her so he's going along with it the plan.

At first I have them argue about the law. She thinks it's ridiculous; he says, "It doesn't matter, it's the law." But after a little of that, the subject is done. So I thought, "Why does she really want to see this play?

She's got the hots for an actor in it." So as the first argument is running out of steam, the young man suddenly says, "Danny's gay, you know." The young woman tries to say it's not about Danny, but the guy knows it is. So the whole tone of the conflict shifts, and we learn something new about the characters. And when that part of the conflict was reaching its limit, I changed it again.

Alterman: Do you find working on ten-minute plays any different from working on one-acts or full-lengths? If so, how?

Pospisil: I tend to look at ten-minute plays as a telling a complete story, but under much different kind of pressure than a longer one-act or full-length play. Take the idea that in a full-length play you have the first five to ten minutes of the show to set up your characters, your story, and the world you're writing about. Then adjust that for a ten-minute play, and you basically have your first page, maybe a page and a half, to do all that. You really have to set the scene and the people involved right away. I'll often start a short play with the characters already in the middle of a conversation or a fight, and then explode that situation to an even greater level of conflict very quickly. There's simply no room for any fat in a ten-minute play.

Alterman: What do you feel constitutes a good ten-minute play?

Pospisil: The elements that make up a good ten-minute play are the same ones that you need to write a good full-length work: characters with a strong want or need, rising stakes or complications that get in the way of that need, a good ear for dialogue, etc. For me a good short play has to have all of that . . . and do it very quickly! The opening of a ten-minute play may be the most important element to my mind. Start the play off with a real bang, and get the audience hooked and interested right away. As I said, the first page of a ten-minute play has to set up the characters, the situation, the world of the story and the style of the piece—comedy, drama, absurdist, etc. It's key to get the audience into the story and get the play moving, so be very focused and economical in what you do in the first minute or so of your short play.

Alterman: What mistakes have you noticed writers make when working on ten-minute plays?

Pospisil: When I teach workshops on writing short plays, the thing I stress is the word "play" in the phrase "ten-minute play." I think a lot of writers focus on the length, and that leads to skits and sketches rather than a play. I love good sketch comedy, but those are really about the situation, not the characters. A sketch is an extended joke. It can be very funny, but in the end the characters aren't really changed. Take a *Saturday Night Live* skit, for example. They often have characters who return in the same situation week after week. Part of the definition of a play is that your protagonist comes up against a conflict that fundamentally changes that person. When I sit down to write I'm usually writing more about a character and how that character deals with whatever problem has come up for him or her, and how that character is changed. I think you can achieve that in a ten-minute play, and it makes them quite magical when they strive to do that.

Alterman: Do you have any additional advice for writers who are about to attempt their first ten-minute play?

Pospisil: Experiment and let your imagination run. It's a short piece; you should try something new, maybe write in a different style than you usually do. It may shed some light on your work in general or even on how you approach writing. I've learned a great deal from writing ten-minute plays. They can really teach you about economy of language, and getting the most out of the limited time that you have to tell the story. I would also highly recommend giving yourself a strict time limit for writing the piece. I think short plays benefit from putting the writer under some pressure—the same way I advocate putting your characters under pressure. I think it can make you write from the gut and take some chances. I've been involved with a number of overnight or "time limited" theater projects, from theAtrainplays to the 24 Hour Plays, and there's really something about only having two to four hours to write something and people who are expecting pages from you at the end of that time. It can make you dig down and go to places in yourself where you may not want to go. But the pressure of that deadline can push you to do that, and come up with something surprising and very good. I have a short play called *It's Not You* that I wrote in less than two hours while riding a New York subway, and going through the breakup of a relationship. It's probably not what I would've written if I'd had more time to think about it, but it's been published in several anthologies, produced over a hundred times and around the world, so I think it's better for the rawness of it.

Mark Harvey Levine

Mark Harvey Levine has had hundreds of productions of his ten-minute plays from New York to Sydney to London. Evenings of his short plays have been produced at the Edinburgh Fringe Festival (*Cabfare for the Common Man*) as well as in Amsterdam, Sao Paulo, New York, Los Angeles, Boston, Indianapolis, Columbus, and other cities.

He has won the Alan Minieri Award, Best Play, and Audience Favorite from New York's 15-Minute Play Festival, and two Best Play honors from the Chester Horn Play Festival (New York, NY). He has twice won Minnesota's Chameleon Theatre Circle's New Play Festival, the Lakeshore Play Festival, and the People's Choice Award at the Annual Play Slam in Ashland, OR. Other awards include the Claire Donaldson Award at the 8 in 48 Festival in Sioux Falls, SD; the Audience Award at the New Works Winter Festival at Acme Theatre in Maynard, MA; as well as many others. More information at www. MarkHarveyLevine.com.

Glenn Alterman: What was it like for you writing your first ten-minute play? Was it your plan to write a ten-minute play, or did it just work out that way?

Mark Harvey Levine: I was lucky and had a very easy time writing my first play. I owe that to getting involved with a theater company that had a writing group. They specialized in ten-minute plays, so that's what I started to write. I was of course nervous about bringing my work in, but the group was incredibly supportive and helpful. When I brought in my work I got very insightful and nonjudgmental critiques. I highly recommend every playwright, whether beginner or not, find a good writing group to join. I don't know if I would have continued writing if I hadn't found such a nurturing environment.

Alterman: Did you come up against any obstacles in writing your first ten-minute play? If so, what were they and how did you overcome them?

Levine: At first, I didn't know what my play was truly about. I had a plot, but no theme. Things happened, but there was no reason for this play to exist, no reason to put it in front of an audience yet. My writing group helped me think about the "why" of the play. A lot of times playwrights—myself included—will have the theme of the play, but not the plot. I had the opposite problem, and it turned out to be a fun problem to solve. I just put my characters in the room and got them talking. Once I did that, I found what I wanted my play to be about. The best way to solve most problems in a play, I've found, is to just keep writing. Eventually your characters will find the solution, and you can throw everything else out.

Alterman: Do you find working on ten-minute plays any different from working on one-acts or full-lengths? If so, how?

Levine: I love working on ten-minute plays because you can hold the whole thing in your head at once. Full-lengths can turn into a morass for me. There are so many directions you can go. With a ten-minute play, you've got a little machine and it all has to work. Also, I like to over-write and then cut back. It's easier to write a 15- or 20-minute play and cut it down to ten minutes then to write a four-hour extravaganza and cut it down to a decent full-length.

Alterman: What do you feel constitutes a good ten-minute play?

Levine: All the things that make a good play of any size have to be there—a beginning, middle, and end (although not necessarily in that order), interesting characters, a compelling story. But in addition, with a ten-minute play you have to be ridiculously concise. There is no room for any fat. I think that's the beauty of the format—it forces you to be ruthless with your writing. You have to cut everything but what is absolutely necessary—no matter how much you love it. It's a good skill to acquire, one that will help you with writing anything.

Alterman: What mistakes have you noticed writers make when working on ten-minute plays?

Levine: I have noticed that a lot of beginning writers will be burning with an idea for a play. Often it will be something autobiographical. But they haven't mastered the form yet, and it is hard to get the same emotion out of the audience that they're feeling about their idea—especially in ten minutes. They end up with a play that is very meaningful to them and incomprehensible to everyone else. I would advise them to put that idea aside—not throw it away, just save it. And work on just writing a good ten-minute play. Try to write about brand-new characters in a brand-new situation. Then, once they've got a few ten-minute plays under their belt, they can go back to that idea they care so much about and, I think, serve it better.

Alterman: Do you have any additional advice for writers who are about to attempt their first ten-minute play?

Levine: As I said before, I highly recommend joining a writers' group. But one of the things I wanted to mention was that the group I happened to join had one very interesting and enlightening rule. No writer was allowed to read his or her own work. Not even the stage directions. Many of the writers in the group were also actors, and they would read your work to you. It is extremely helpful, and occasionally mortifying, to hear your own words read back to you by good actors. You can see where you've gone on too long—and most everyone goes on too long in a first draft. You can hear which lines get an unexpected laugh, and which lines lie there like a dead tuna. But mostly you can hear how little you need, sometimes, to get your point across. So that is my biggest recommendation. Somehow, somewhere, find actors to read your play to you. And this is equally important: develop the ability to really listen to your own play. Don't be so in love with it that you can't hear where it's dragging or falling flat. Try to hear it as a brand-new audience member.

Arlene Hutton

Arlene Hutton is a three-time winner of the Samuel French Short Play Festival and a six-time Heideman Award finalist. Her first one-act, *I Dream Before I Take the Stand*, which premiered at the Edinburgh Fringe Festival, is published by Playscripts and appears in several anthologies. She is best known for *The Nibroc Trilogy*, which includes *Last Train to Nibroc* (Drama League nomination for Best Play), *See Rock City* (In the Spirit of America Award), and *Gulf View Drive* (*LA Weekly* Theater Award nomination and Ovation Award nomination), all published by Dramatists Play Service.

An alumna of New Dramatists, Hutton is a member of the Dramatists Guild and Ensemble Studio Theatre. Her plays have been presented Off and Off-Off-Broadway, regionally, in London, and around the world.

Glenn Alterman: What was it like for you writing your first ten-minute play?

Arlene Hutton: I was an actor and director first and began writing short plays to create roles for myself and my friends. My first plays were short and came out in a rush, partly because for several years I had been performing competitive improv, which was a natural progression to playwriting.

Alterman: Was it your plan to write a ten-minute play, or did it just work out that way?

Hutton: Ten minutes seems to be just the amount of time needed to tell a story with a beginning, middle, and end. Although I didn't set out to write ten-minute plays, most of my short works fall into that time frame. If a play comes in at twelve minutes it can usually be cut to ten and is all the better for the edits.

Alterman: Did you come up against any obstacles in writing your first ten-minute play? If so, what were they and how did you overcome them?

Hutton: Well, I'd like to say there were many obstacles and I heroically rose to the occasion and fought my inner demons and overcame my fears, winning many battles; but to be honest, writing, performing, and producing short plays has taken me on the best journeys of my life and I'm happiest when I'm working on one, either writing or in the rehearsal room making the final changes.

Oddly enough, my earlier plays were easier to write, coming out fully formed, starting with an idea or a character and writing a first draft in one or two sittings. I even dreamed one play and wrote it immediately upon waking up. The challenges came later; acquired skill and knowledge led to judgment and self-consciousness. To overcome that I try to write the first draft as quickly as possible and do revisions after hearing actors read and respond to the work. I do a lot more rewriting now.

The biggest obstacle as a new playwright was getting produced and I solved that by presenting my short plays myself, first at the Edinburgh Festival Fringe and then at the first two years of the New York Fringe Festival. Self-producing jump started my career.

Some of America's best playwrights wrote short plays early in their careers—Tennessee Williams, Thornton Wilder.

Alterman: Do you find working on ten-minute plays any different from working on one-acts or full-lengths? If so, how?

Hutton: Ten-minute plays are instant gratification! A full-length play may not only take years to research and write, but can get stuck in readings and development for a long time before being produced. Theater companies often invite or commission ten-minute plays that are to be fully staged only a month or two later, and that's lots of fun, to go so quickly from page to performance.

For several years I was privileged to be a writer for the Atrain-plays, a 24-hour format where plays written while riding public transportation are presented off-book in front of an audience the very next day. Those were great events and the speed of creation was part of the experience.

I like to think of full-length plays as a series of one-acts, and I write each scene for a longer play as if it were basically a ten-minute play.

Alterman: What do you feel constitutes a good ten-minute play?

Hutton: It is about one thing, one moment in time, one issue, one conflict, a perfect miniature. The play starts in the middle of the conflict, joining a conversation already in progress. Like good improv, everything mentioned in the beginning gets reincorporated by the end. Something changes and the ending should be surprising but inevitable.

Alterman: What mistakes have you noticed writers make when working on ten-minute plays?

Hutton:
- The script doesn't have page numbers.
- The play is a sketch, or an idea, rather than a play.
- The play is actually a 12- or 15-minute play wearing the costume of a smaller font and masquerading as a shorter work.
- The play has multiple scenes. Sometimes that can work, but in general it's best to have the play take place in real time.
- The play takes too long getting to the point. The first page or two of the first draft are usually about the playwright getting to know the characters.
- The story doesn't answer the Passover question: why is this day different?
- Too much of the dialogue is spoken subtext; actors can bring so much to the piece through behavior.
- The play is an argument instead of a conflict.
- The characters are only talking instead of doing.
- The play has a promising beginning and a disappointing ending.
- The play ends too cleverly, with an unjustified surprise or twist that has no setup.
- The play is really a bigger story crammed into ten pages.
- The script has technical challenges that make it impossible to produce in an evening of other one-act plays.

- The play hasn't had enough revisions. An eight-page play can go through eight drafts, each one fine-tuning the conflict, language, and characters. There is no margin for error in a ten-minute play. The key to a good ten-minute play is rewrite, rewrite, rewrite.

Alterman: Do you have any additional advice for writers who are about to attempt their first ten-minute play?

Hutton: Read lots of plays. Go see evenings of one-act plays. Attend the Samuel French Short Play Festival. Deadlines are good; get together with other writers and create an event for yourselves. Have fun writing plays for specific actors. Write the first draft as quickly as you can, and then see what happens when you cut the first two pages.

Alex Broun

Alex Broun is one of the world's most performed ten-minute playwrights. Since he began writing ten-minute plays in the late 1990s he has had nearly 100 different ten-minute plays produced in over 800 productions. His most popular ten-minute play, *10,000 Cigarettes*, has been produced over 150 times. To date his work has been performed in no fewer than 26 countries and translated into three languages. His Web site, www.alexbroun.com, where you can download and perform many of his plays free of charge, is one of the most popular websites in the world for ten-minute plays and has recorded over 10 million hits.

Glenn Alterman: What was it like for you writing your first ten-minute play? Was it your plan to write a ten-minute play, or did it just work out that way?

Alex Broun: I wrote my first ten-minute play without actually knowing I was writing a ten-minute play. I was living in South Africa in the late 1990s and I became interested in writing a suite of short plays all set on New Year's Eve, with each play set in a different country. Many of my most popular ten-minute plays, like *The First Fireworks* and *Saturday Night Newtown, Sunday Morning Enmore* were written as a part of that project. But even then I loved the economy of stage time and compressing the action of the play into a very short time frame.

Alterman: Did you come up against any obstacles in writing your first ten-minute play? If so, what were they and how did you overcome them?

Broun: The writing of my first ten-minute plays came surprisingly easy to me. The situations, characters, and even dialogue seemed to spring fully formed into my mind. It was just a matter of putting what was in my head on paper.

Alterman: Do you find working on ten-minute plays any different from working on one-acts or full-lengths? If so, how?

Broun: The wonderful thing about writing a ten-minute play is that you can write a first draft in a burst of a few hours. A full-length play may take months or years to write, and people with a busy schedule don't often find the time. But you can write a ten-minute play in an afternoon or an evening. In a ten-minute play you can also explore an interesting situation or set of characters that may not hold for a full-length play. It is incredibly difficult to write a play that sustains an audience's attention for a full night of theater, but I think it's achievable for everybody to write a good ten-minute play. People used to say everyone has a novel in them. I'm not sure that's the case, but I do think everyone has a good ten-minute play inside them. It's just a matter of letting it come out on to the paper.

Alterman: What do you feel constitutes a good ten-minute play?

Broun: The same thing that makes a good long play: interesting characters, good dialogue, and an absorbing situation or story. The trick is knowing how big a story to tell or situation to explore in your play. If you choose too slight a story or situation, the play will come off like a skit; and if you choose too large a story or situation, it will come off underdone. You need to choose a story or situation that you can satisfactorily explore or tell in a ten-minute framework.

Alterman: What mistakes have you noticed writers make when working on ten-minute plays?

Broun: The most common mistake I find is that writers write short films rather than short plays. We are so bombarded by TV, film, and screen images in the modern world that it's really hard to think in stage. Try to visualize your play happening on stage, rather than film.

Think about what you can write that will be interesting for actors to act, directors to direct, and an audience to watch. Our job as playwrights is to make the *doing* as interesting as possible for the people *watching*. Other mistakes are clumsy dialogue or too much exposition in the dialogue. Ask yourself, would your characters really say that?

Also often writers have interesting situations or starting points, but then they don't explore them. To write a good ten-minute play you have to have a good idea, but you also have to execute it well. So many ten-minute plays start with a good idea but the writer doesn't execute it well.

Alterman: Do you have any additional advice you have for writers who are about to attempt their first ten-minute play?

Broun: Turn off the inner critic and just start writing. You don't know what you'll come up with unless you try. And remember, very few scripts come out perfect the first time. You can go back and revise your play later on, but you need to get something down on paper first. That first draft will be the raw material that you use to shape your play, the mound of clay from which the finished sculpture will emerge. So just write it!

Rich Orloff

Rich Orloff is a prolific author of short plays (mostly comedies), which have had over 800 productions on six continents (and a staged reading in Antarctica). The plays have been published in *The Art of the One-Act*, *The Bedford Introduction to Literature*, three editions of the annual *Best Ten-Minute Plays* series, and five editions of the annual *Best American Short Plays*. Playscripts has published 60 of his short plays in eight volumes. He's also written a dozen award-winning, full-length comedies. For more information, see www.richorloff.com.

Glenn Alterman: What was it like for you writing your first ten-minute play? Was it your plan to write a ten-minute play, or did it just work out that way?

Rich Orloff: I wrote my first pair of short plays in the early 1980s, shortly after I joined a playwriting workshop in Los Angeles run by the wonderfully nurturing playwright Oliver Hailey. This was when the ten-minute play form was just beginning to get attention, and the workshop had just gotten acclaim for *24 Hours*, a production of 24 short plays (in two parts), each one set during a different hour of the day.

I was a novice playwright then, eager to write plays but overwhelmed by the challenge. As I watched that production, I remembered conversations between my mom and my grandmother, which developed into a quiet, slice-of-life comedy called *Gram Folds the Laundry*. Meanwhile, Oliver was planning a new production of plays, each set during a different month of the year. I wasn't sure if Oliver would like my play, but I didn't know what else to write. A friend jokingly suggested I write a play with lots of attractive women in it. From that remark, I got the idea for *Four Extremely Attractive Women Sitting Around Fantasizing About Rich Orloff*.

Ever since then, I've loved the form and its possibilities, either for capturing a moment in time, as in *Gram*, or getting a crazy notion and running with it, as in *Four Women*.

Alterman: Did you come up against any obstacles in writing your first ten-minute play? If so, what were they and how did you overcome them?

Orloff: As with writing plays of any length, both plays went through several drafts of shaping and toning. I moved moments around, so that the action in the plays would continue to build. I cut moments I liked but which proved to be extraneous. Ten-minute plays don't allow for any fat.

Alterman: Do you find working on ten-minute plays any different from working on one-acts or full-lengths? If so, how?

Orloff: The biggest difference is that I get to type "THE END" months earlier than I do for a full-length. Writing a play of any length takes commitment, and I'm never sure how long that commitment will take. It can feel great creating a draft of a short play relatively quickly and having something to look at.

Alterman: What do you feel constitutes a good ten-minute play?

Orloff: The best short plays *usually* start with a situation the audience can grasp quickly (even if the situation turns out to be different from what is initially assumed), engages the audience in its journey, and has a surprising twist near the end. The surprise can be moving or comedic, but it shouldn't just be about plot. It should reflect on the theme and story that have built to that moment.

Alterman: What mistakes have you noticed writers make working on ten-minute plays?

Orloff: The first mistake is probably the most obvious: Just as a short story is different from a novel, a short play is different from a full-length. The story should fit the length, instead of someone cramming a story into ten minutes just to create a ten-minute play. *Death of a Salesman* is not a good idea for a ten-minute play. A short play should feel like a fully developed piece and not a synopsis for a longer play.

A common mistake in comedies: There's a difference between a play (which has characters and an arc, regardless of length) and a sketch (where the main goal is to be funny). I've written both, and many of my comedies are a blend of the two. I usually search for an arc to my story, even in something that seems like a sketch. I always try to remember which form I'm working in, and I make different decisions based on what mix of play and sketch I'm writing. Sometimes I watch a short comedy, and I think, "The playwright hasn't decided what form this is." All plays create worlds, and all worlds have rules. Know the world of your play.

Alterman: Do you have any additional advice for writers who are about to attempt their first ten-minute play?

Orloff: First and foremost, have fun! Why not?

Beyond that, my main advice to a writer about to write his or her first short play is to write at least four or five. You'll learn along the way, and you'll discover what works and doesn't work for you. One of the pleasures in writing a short play is that I get to work in different genres and explore different ideas. My collection *Couples* includes a light comedy (*Matterhorn*), a topical satire (*Oh Happy Day*), a Pinteresque piece (*Lion Tamer*), a poetic monologue (*Invisible Woman*), a drama inspired by the works of Edward Hopper (*Afternoon Sun*), an irreverent comedy about a usually serious subject (*Right Sensation*), a drama inspired by a true story I heard (*Class Dismissed*), and a play where my main goal was to let my bile out (*Heart of Fire*). Eight different worlds and moods. Writing these plays stretched me, and I've used what I've learned when I write my full-lengths.

A few basic bits of advice:

- Hear the play aloud. I inevitably learn things about my plays by hearing them that I'd never learn just by reading them. Key things I listen for include when a play drags or when a sentence is difficult for an actor to say.
- When you've revised the play, hear the play aloud again. You'll still learn things.
- Get feedback. You don't have to agree with it, and you shouldn't *always* agree with it. But if several people have problems with something, listen to them. They may be wrong with their diagnosis, but there's probably something behind what they say.

- Have fun! Agony just gets in the way.
- Learn what the most conducive creative environment is for you. I write on a chair or a couch, not at my desk. (Too much pressure!) I write my rough drafts on "used" paper (otherwise headed for the recycling heap). I tried writing a play a couple of years ago on lined paper. It didn't work as well. It might for you, but not for me. Everyone develops their own technique.
- Finally, have fun! The audience hopes to have fun, whether it's to be amused or moved or even devastated by what they see on stage. You're entitled to have fun, too.

Chapter 11

Interviews with Producers of Ten-Minute Plays

Kate Snodgrass

Artistic Director, Boston Theater Marathon
and Boston Playwright's Theater

Kate Snodgrass is the artistic director of both the Elliot Norton Award–winning Boston Theater Marathon and Boston Playwrights' Theatre, the "Home of New Plays in Boston." The author of the Actors Theatre of Louisville's Heideman Award–winning play *Haiku*, she has been recognized with two IRNE Awards for Best New Play and a nomination for the American Theatre Critics Association's Steinberg Award for Best New Play. She lectures in Playwriting in the Boston University Graduate School and is a member of AEA, AFTRA, and the Dramatists Guild. Acknowledged by Boston's StageSource in 2001 as a "Theatre Hero," Kate is a former National Chair of Playwriting at the Kennedy Center American College Theater Festival; she received the KCACTF's inaugural Milan Stitt Award as an Outstanding Teacher of Playwriting. Kate is a Playwriting Fellow at the Huntington Theatre Company.

Glenn Alterman: Where did the idea of a ten-minute play festival for your theater come from? Why did you feel it would be successful?

Kate Snodgrass: The idea came from two serendipitous things. First, I had participated in the Circle Repertory Theatre Company's fund-raiser "The All Day Sucker" in New York a couple of years earlier (I think there were 40 plays involved in that day—and it was supposed to last 10 hours; it lasted 14). Second, my friend Bill Lattanzi and I wanted to get playwrights involved with producers in Boston. We melded the two ideas into one and opted to have *all* the theater companies (40 then, now 50) involved in producing. We didn't want to stump for just one theater company—we wanted the community to be involved. What's good for the community is good for playwrights.

We had no idea if it would be successful, but we were desperate. Surprisingly, after our first press release, the newspapers were calling *us*, not the other way around. It was an idea whose time had come, and it was standing room only from the first hour.

Alterman: Are ten-minute play festivals difficult to produce and coordinate?

Snodgrass: Not any more, but it takes organizing. When we began with 40 plays (now we do 50 in ten hours), we flew by the seat of our pants at Boston Playwrights' Theatre—with all the proceeds going to charity (this is still true). We had two small theater spaces at our disposal, so we performed the plays twice each (once in each theater). The scenes changes were coordinated; we had two stage managers and two run crews. If the audience sat in one theater all day long, they could see all the plays; and the playwrights could move back and forth to see both of their performances. Now we stay in one larger venue and perform only once in that theater. It's easier on our staff and the run crews, too. It's not as "exciting" (read, scary), but it works like clockwork, because our technical staff is impeccable. Five plays per hour—we're always on time with minutes to spare!

Alterman: In general, what do you think of ten-minute plays?

Snodgrass: I love them. Not only do audiences adore them—they're like crackerjacks; you can't eat just one—but they're wonderful teaching tools. How to make one thing happen within a given amount of time—dramatists have to know how to do this. The ten-minute play requires dramatic action.

Alterman: Do you think they're easier or more difficult for playwrights to write?

Snodgrass: They are deceptive. We think we can do it easily—anybody can write ten pages, right? But the genre calls for focus, imagination, and a superior understanding of the three-dimensional space. The ten-minute play is a mini full-length play with all the Aristotelian elements in full force (in absurdist works, too), just truncated into ten minutes. "Just" is the deceptive word here. It sounds easy, but it requires craft.

Alterman: How do you decide which plays will be included in your festivals?

Snodgrass: Our plays—we get over 400 entries every year from all over New England—are read by three people from our theater community (i.e., audience members, actors, directors, designers, producers, you name them) and scored. The highest-scored plays get sent on to a final team of three readers who pick the final 50 plays. These readers are not the same every year, but they are always theater professionals giving of their time. We also offer several playwrights a place in the Boston Theater Marathon—writers like Israel Horovitz, Theresa Rebeck, Robert Brustein, etc. (the list changes every year). These playwrights have earned their place in our community and across the nation.

Alterman: What kind of feedback do you get from your audiences about your ten-minute play festivals?

Snodgrass: We get kudos all around. The Boston Theater Marathon is now a tradition on the Boston theater scene. We showcase literally hundreds of actors and directors, and 50 playwrights get their works performed every year. We are acknowledged by the Boston area newspapers in features and reviews, and anthologies of the BTM are published—first by Samuel French, and now by Smith & Kraus Publishers.

Alterman: Do you have any advice for playwrights who want to write ten-minute plays and get them produced?

Snodgrass: First, write one. See for yourself how difficult and how easy it is. Then I'd band together with other writers, talk some actors into giving you a break, and produce an evening of ten-minute plays (don't wait for somebody else to acknowledge you; use your power). Invite all and sundry. Word of mouth is the answer to everything in the theater, and audiences want to participate. An evening of ten-minute plays is never boring, and, done right, the ten-minute play pushes the boundaries of theater as we know it.

Alice Walker

Contest Director, Theatre Oxford's National Ten-Minute Play Contest Producer, Theatre Oxford's Ten-Minute Play Festival

Alice Walker is a vibrant member of the arts community in Oxford, Mississippi. She currently serves on the board of directors for the Yoknapatawpha Arts Council as well as the board for VOX Press. She is a member of the board of directors for Theatre Oxford, Oxford's community theater, and serves as the organization's managing producer.

She is also contest director for Theatre Oxford's National Ten-Minute Play Contest and producer for the Annual Ten-Minute Play Festival.

Glenn Alterman: Where did the idea of a ten-minute play festival for your theater come from? Why did you feel it would be successful?

Alice Walker: Local playwrights, Neil White and L. W. Thomas, founded the National Ten-Minute Play Contest in 1998. The first grand prize winner was produced in 1999 prior to the production of Neil White's play *Paper*. The Annual Ten-Minute Play Festival started in 2000 and featured the grand prize winner from the national contest and locally written plays. The Annual Ten-Minute Play Festival was and still is an ideal way to showcase local playwrights and excite local audiences about productions.

Alterman: Are ten-minute play festivals difficult to produce and coordinate?

Walker: The most difficult thing about producing a ten-minute play festival is being in charge of a large number of people. On average, I oversee five different directors and five different casts. That means I am dealing with five different rehearsal schedules, as well as different set and technical needs, props, and costumes. The key is staying organized so all the plays come together as one complete show.

   The good thing about producing a ten-minute play festival is that the whole rehearsal process can be done in a short amount of time. Since a single rehearsal for a ten-minute play is typically not that long, directors can coordinate with each other and schedule one- to two-hour rehearsal slots, say every other day, and have plenty of rehearsal time. Blocking for directors and getting off book for actors takes a lot less time than with a full-length play, so a festival can go up in just a few weeks.

Alterman: In general, what do you think of ten-minute plays?

Walker: I personally love ten-minute plays. The ten-minute play is a wonderful exercise for first-time playwrights, or experienced playwrights, for that matter. A ten-minute play festival is also an excellent way to bring in first-time directors and actors. My favorite thing about producing a ten-minute play festival is the overwhelming number of community members who get involved.

Alterman: Do you think they're easier or more difficult for playwrights to write?

Walker: I wouldn't say that a ten-minute play is easier or more difficult to write. In both a ten-minute play and a full-length play, the playwright has to think about the same things—characters, dialogue, plot, etc. The structure is the same for both—setup, conflict, and resolution. The ten-minute playwright just has to execute in a shorter amount of time.

When you are dealing with a ten-page script, it is important to keep things moving. A ten-minute play can seem much shorter than ten minutes if the pacing is good. Otherwise, a ten-minute play can feel like an eternity. For example, a lot of long monologues in a ten-minute play makes it seem longer and often times boring. A talent for editing and being able to create swift-moving dialogue is necessary to write a successful ten-minute play.

Alterman: How do you decide which plays will be included in your festivals?

Walker: Theatre Oxford produces the grand prize winner from the national contest at our annual festival. Four or five plays written by local playwrights are also produced. These local plays are selected either from previous submissions to the national contest or from submissions made directly to the theater for consideration. The local plays are often workshopped before they are produced at the annual festival.

Alterman: What kind of feedback do you get from your audiences about your ten-minute play festivals?

Walker: The Annual Ten-Minute Play Festival is Theatre Oxford's most well-attended production. Audiences seem to love the format. A night of five or six ten-minute plays easily keeps an audience's attention. It's been jokingly said that if you don't like one play, wait ten minutes and there'll be another one!

For a small community theater, the large number of actors, directors, and crew involved brings in lots of audience members, not to mention playwrights and their family and friends who attend. I hear from many audience members, year after year, that the Ten-Minute Play Festival is their favorite production of the year.

Alterman: Do you have any advice for playwrights who want to write ten-minute plays and get them produced?

Walker: If you want to write a ten-minute play, remember to keep it simple. One scene and a minimal set seem to work best. Ten-minute plays with scene changes generally do not work. I have seen ten-minute plays with a split stage, going from one scene on stage right to another on stage left, that have worked well, but those plays are still challenging to pull off. Use as few characters as possible. Two to four characters is a good guideline, although some contests require three characters.

Remember, a ten-minute play needs to be compact. Think of it as a mini sitcom, or mini drama, as the case may be. Dialogue is extremely important and needs to have a quick pace and flow well. Try to stay away from lots of long monologues that may slow down the pace or bore the audience.

Keeping it simple does not mean the concept has to be simple. The idea for a ten-minute play can be very abstract. In fact, the ten-minute play format lends itself to abstract subject matter. I have produced ten-minute plays about world leaders playing a game of Monopoly, about ghosts and talking to the dead, and several plays with animals and superheroes as the characters. No subject matter is really off limits when it comes to a ten-minute play.

Feedback is beneficial when writing a ten-minute play. If you can, conduct a workshop for your script by inviting actors and other play-wrights to a read-through and take suggestions afterward.

There are many ten-minute play contests across the country. Most contests have a small entry fee, and some award a cash prize to the winner. Submit to as many contests as you can. Also, look into ten-minute play festivals in your area and how to submit your play to be produced. Don't be afraid of rejection. Just keep writing!

Seth Gordon

Associate Artistic Director, Repertory Theatre of St. Louis

Seth Gordon is the associate artistic director of the Repertory Theatre of St. Louis, the main professional theater in its region and the largest professional theater in Missouri. Previously Mr. Gordon was associate artistic director of the Cleveland Play House and associate producer of Primary Stages in New York. He has directed plays at these and many other theaters, including Studio Arena Theatre, Syracuse Stage, Stages Repertory in Houston, and many small theaters in New York, including Ensemble Studio Theatre and Theatre for the New City. He created the New American Writers Group at Primary Stages and has directed and/or produced countless readings of new plays by many of the US's leading playwrights.

Glenn Alterman: Where did the idea of a ten-minute play festival for your theater come from? Why did you feel it would be successful?

Seth Gordon: The first ten-minute play festival, which, by the way, you participated in, was created at Primary Stages in New York, when I was associate producer in the 1990s. It started when Primary Stages applied for a grant to commission a play about the environment. When we didn't get the grant we decided to look for ways to talk with our audience about the issue in ways that wouldn't have the costs of a commission and full production, and the idea of a reading series of plays written especially for the occasion came up. We decided to call it the Planet Project and proceeded to write to about 50 playwrights inviting them to participate. We told them they could take any approach they wished, as long as the play was ten minutes and written especially for us. We told them there was no fee attached but that participation was invitation only and if they wrote us a play we would include it. The list included every writer we'd worked with, along with many of our favorites. We received about twenty-five entries and read them all over three nights. The project was far more successful than anticipated, and so the following year we did the Legacy Project, a reading series of plays about where we're from, with similar results. The Planet Project was 1995, the Legacy Project was 1996, and the New York Project, the last of these, was 1997.

Alterman: Are ten-minute play festivals difficult to produce/coordinate?

Gordon: They have their particular challenges that are different from producing a full-length play. Also, when we did these projects we only did readings, not full productions. The degree of difficulty will depend on how many plays are being done, the level of production being attempted, and the degree to which the writers are working on the plays up to opening.

Alterman: In general, what do you think of ten-minute plays?

Gordon: I have mixed feelings about them. When done well they can be quite beautiful, but most frankly seem underwritten to me. When we did our projects they were quite successful, and some of the plays were very good, but the success was measured by the participation of the playwrights and audience response, not necessarily by the level of writing we inspired.

Alterman: Do you think they're easier or more difficult for playwrights to write?

Gordon: My guess is they are more difficult because of the creative limitations involved.

Alterman: How do you decide which plays will be included in your festivals?

Gordon: In the festivals we've produced, we handpicked participants and guaranteed that their play would be selected if they wrote it especially for the festival. In the case of a festival that has open submissions my guess would be that the selection process would be about the same regardless of the length of the play.

Alterman: What kind of feedback do you get from your audiences about your ten-minute play festivals?

Gordon: The feedback was uniformly positive, though the positive response was about the level of playwright involved, the volume of plays, and the communal feeling engendered by the very large number of theater artists coming together for one project.

Alterman: Do you have any advice for playwrights who want to write ten-minute plays and get them produced?

Gordon: My feeling is that most producers are not looking for ten-minute plays, unless they happen to be. I would suggest writing plays when you know that someone is looking for them. Otherwise my experience is that ten-minute plays tend not to be produced, or at least they tend not to be produced in a manner that provides a fee for the author.

Chapter 12

Interviews with Publishers of Ten-Minute Plays

Sarah Bernstein

Playscripts

Sarah Bernstein joined the Playscripts literary department in May 2009 and was promoted to literary manager in 2011. As literary manager, she oversees the ongoing development of Playscripts' acquisitions strategy and review process, and works with playwrights, agents, and artistic directors to establish successful partnerships between artists and Playscripts. She has also worked in the finance and business affairs departments at the Weinstein Company and currently serves on the literary wing of the Lark Play Development Center. Sarah received a BA in literary arts from Brown University, where she studied playwriting with Paula Vogel.

Glenn Alterman: What do you look for when deciding which ten-minute play you'll choose to publish?

Sarah Bernstein: We're looking for plays that are both high quality and high impact. A powerfully funny or powerfully moving ten-minute play reaches an audience with a kind of directness and clarity that even excellent full-lengths can't always achieve. It's a unique medium in that respect. We want to publish the kind of short plays that have a lingering effect belying their brevity.

Because the market for ten-minute plays is smaller than it is for one-acts or full-lengths, we are especially drawn to plays that have the potential to be performed by a variety of groups. There are plays in our

Great Short Plays and Great Short Comedies collections that have been performed at professional theaters, colleges, high schools, and community theaters all over the world.

Alterman: What things are definite "turnoffs" when reading plays you're considering?

Bernstein: When writing a ten-minute play, simplicity and clarity are paramount, but this doesn't mean you can coast on a good premise or hang all your ambitions on one funny twist. Many of the short plays we decline to publish have a promising conceit but fail to keep a reader or audience engaged from start to finish.

Alterman: Is there much of a demand these days from theaters and theater companies for ten-minute plays and evenings of ten-minute plays? If so, why do you think that is?

Bernstein: Just about every college with a drama department is in need of strong short plays, as these make excellent projects for first-time directors. We regularly license ten-minute plays to colleges and find that they are often interested in our more challenging material.

Our *Great Shorts* collections sell extremely well to both high schools and colleges. Even if the plays are only being used for in-class scene work, it means increased exposure (not to mention book royalties) for our playwrights.

Community and professional theaters will rarely produce a standalone ten-minute play, but many stage evenings of ten-minute plays. A theater might produce several short works from the same playwright, or they'll sometimes present a collection of ten-minute pieces on a single theme. Your ten-minute play about dating, aging, or politics might catch the eye of a theater looking to build an evening of similar shorts.

Alterman: Many ten-minute plays are really just ten-minute "sketches." What do you feel are the main differences between the two?

Bernstein: Many of the plays I referred to earlier, those with strong premises and spotty execution, could be called sketches. A play, whatever its length, is more than a vehicle for a clever joke or idea. Whether you are writing an absurd comedy or a wrenching drama, you should do the bidding of your characters and not the other way around.

Alterman: What advice do you have for playwrights who want to write ten-minute plays?

Bernstein: I think writing ten-minute plays is a fantastic exercise for playwrights. It strengthens your powers of focus and precision in ways that benefit all of your writing. Read (and see) as many ten-minute plays of varied content and style as you can. Note what works and what doesn't. Why do some plays leave you exhilarated and other plays leave you dissatisfied? A good way to start building your catalogue of ten-minute plays is to write specifically for one of the excellent ten-minute play contests held annually in the US. Both the deadlines and the requirements of these contests can help spur you to write. For example, the ten-minute play contest held every year by Actors Theatre of Louisville now requires that all characters in your play be between 18 and 28 years old. You may never have planned to write about this particular demographic, but stepping outside your comfort zone can produce unexpected and exciting results.

Geri Albrecht

Heuer Publishing

Geri Albrecht is editor in chief of Heuer Publishing, where she edited Eddie McPherson's best-selling play *Virgil's Wedding* and many other short and full-length plays. She helped to launch Green Room Scripts, an online self-publishing service started in 2012, and Dominion Publications, an online book publisher and distributor. Green Room Scripts is considered by many to be a model of self-publishing for theater, and a pioneer in developing and publishing anthologies for classroom and performance use. Albrecht is a member of Theatre Cedar Rapids, which is among the nation's largest and longest-running community theaters.

Glenn Alterman: What do you look for when deciding which ten-minute play you'll choose to publish?

Geri Albrecht: Good ten-minute plays require the same dramatic elements that exist in full-length plays; however, they must be more compact, dynamic, and resourceful. There is no time to waste. We look for the initial incident, the rise of action, climax, and conclusion. We expect to see vibrant character and emotive language, but yes, we still need a solid plot.

Alterman: What things are definite "turnoffs" when reading plays you're considering?

Albrecht: It's a deal-breaker when I can't tell one character from another. I've read my share of ten-minute plays, and there's nothing worse than bland, vanilla characters. Instead give me characters that demand my attention, characters that I want to know. I know they're not perfect, and that's what makes them perfectly interesting. Another turnoff would be overly complicated plots with multiple scenes. No, thanks.

Alterman: Is there much of a demand these days from theaters and theater companies for ten-minute plays and evenings of ten-minute plays? If so, why do you think that is?

Albrecht: Yes, I think there is serious demand for ten-minute theater. We've seen a tremendous demand for ten-minute plays at competitive thespian festivals (forensics, speech and debate), and growing interest at the high school level. Why? Broader involvement, arts-integrated classrooms; and the form itself is quick, pithy, and concise, something that is embraced and easily consumed by the digital generation. Community theaters are also beginning to embrace ten-minute theater, Reasons vary from increasing their volunteer and audience base, lower cost, flexibility in casting and rehearsal schedules, and improved quality of ten-minute theater.

Alterman: Many ten-minute plays are really just ten-minute "sketches." What do you feel are the main differences between the two?

Albrecht: Aristotle's basic elements of drama obtain for a good ten-minute play as they do for a good full-length play. The common mistake made by writers of ten-minute plays is that they tend to skip or overly abbreviate important elements, especially theme or thought, plot and action, language and rhythm, and reduce the play to nothing more than a sketch. That said, there is nothing wrong with a good sketch, much as there is nothing wrong with a good vaudeville act, as they both can be entertaining. However they tend to lack the ability to evoke emotion and stir thought.

Alterman: What advice do you have for playwrights who want to write ten-minute plays?

Albrecht: The most successful writers will construct a plot that allows the drama to flow quickly, emphasize language to color their characters, allow their characters to show more than they tell, maintain a strong central theme/thought (you don't have time to manage subplots), and deliver something unique and completely irresistible to the audience (and to the editor).

Lawrence Harbison

Smith & Kraus Publishers

Lawrence Harbison was in charge of new play acquisition for Samuel French, Inc., for over 30 years, during which time his work on behalf of playwrights resulted in the first publication of such subsequent luminaries as Jane Martin, Don Nigro, Tina Howe, Theresa Rebeck, José Rivera, William Mastrosimone, Charles Fuller, and Ken Ludwig, among many others; and the acquisition of musicals such as *Smoke of the Mountain, A . . . My Name Is Alice, Little Shop of Horrors*, and *Three Guys Naked from the Waist Down*. He is now a freelance editor, primarily for Smith & Kraus, Inc., for whom he edits annual anthologies of best plays by new playwrights and women playwrights, best ten-minute plays, and best monologues and scenes for men and for women. For many years he wrote a weekly column on his adventures in the theater for two Manhattan newspapers, the *Chelsea Clinton News* and the *Westsider*. His new column, "On the Aisle with Larry," is a weekly feature at www.smithandkraus.com.

He works with individual playwrights to help them develop their plays (see his Web site, www.playfixer.com). He has also served as literary manager or literary consultant for several theaters, such as Urban Stages and American Jewish Theatre. He is a member of both the Outer Critics Circle and the Drama Desk. He has served many times over the years as a judge and commentator for various national play contests and lectures regularly at colleges and universities. He holds a BA from Kenyon College and an MA from the University of Michigan.

*To begin the interview, Mr. Harbison requested that I include the following foreword from his book, *The Best Ten-Minute Plays, 2011* (Smith & Kraus).

In years past, playwrights who were just starting out wrote one-act plays of 30 to 40 minutes in duration. One thinks of writers such as A. R. Gurney, Lanford Wilson, John Guare, and several others. Now, new playwrights tend to work in the ten-minute play genre, largely because there are so many production opportunities. Twenty or so years ago, there were none. I was senior editor for Samuel French at that time, and it occurred to me that there might be a market for these very short plays. Actors Theatre of Louisville had been commissioning them for several years, for use by their Apprentice Company, and they assisted me in compiling an anthology of their plays, which did so well that Samuel French has published several more anthologies of ten-minute plays from ATL. For the first time, ten-minute plays were now published and widely available, and they started getting produced. There are now many ten-minute play festivals every year, not only in the U.S. but all over the world.

What makes a good ten-minute play? Well, first and foremost I have to like it. Isn't that what we mean when we call a play, a film, a novel "good?" We mean that it effectively portrays the world as I see it. Aside from this obvious fact, a good ten-minute play has to have the same elements that any good play must have: a strong conflict; interesting, well-drawn characters; and compelling subject matter. It also has to have a clear beginning, middle, and end. In other words, it's a full-length play which runs about ten minutes. Many of the plays which are submitted to me are scenes, not complete plays; well-written scenes in many cases, but scenes nonetheless. They leave me wanting more. I chose plays which are complete in and of themselves, which I believe will excite those of you who produce ten-minute plays; because if a play isn't produced, it's the proverbial sound of a tree falling in the forest far away.

Glenn Alterman: What do you look for when deciding which ten-minute play you'll choose to publish?

Lawrence Harbison: A full-length play in about ten minutes with a unique voice.

Alterman: What things are definite "turnoffs" when reading plays you're considering?

Harbison: Nothing "definite"—just the same things that make any play good.

Alterman: Is there much of a demand these days from theaters and theater companies for ten-minute plays and evenings of ten-minute plays? If so, why do you think that is?

Harbison: Yes. Easy to produce.

Alterman: Many ten-minute plays are really just ten-minute "sketches." What do you feel are the main differences between the two?

Harbison: My point is that a good ten-minute play is a full-length (i.e., complete) play which runs about ten minutes. Many ten-minute plays seem like scenes from a larger work (in fact, many of them are).

Alterman: What advice do you have for playwrights who want to write ten-minute plays?

Harbison: Go ahead and write them.

Chapter 13

Three Successful Ten-Minute Plays

The Popcorn Sonata

by Jenny Lyn Bader

The Popcorn Sonata was first performed at Primary Stages in New York, directed by Casey Childs, with Anne O'Sullivan and Margot White, in the event "A Moment of Bliss," curated by Tyler Marchant. Its world premiere production was at Café Theatre at George St. Playhouse in New Jersey, produced by David Hoffman, directed by Julie Kramer, with Amy Clites and Gloria Garayua, with music composed by Matthew Aidekman. It had its regional premiere at City Theatre in Florida, directed by Susan Dempsey, with Kim Ostrenko and Lauren Feldman. Other credits include production in 0 at Henlopen Theatre in Delaware and Stamford Fringe Festival in Connecticut, both directed by Ari Laura Kreith, and at NYU/Strasberg, directed by Julie Kramer. It was published in *2004: The Best 10-Minute Plays for Two Actors* (Smith & Kraus), ed. Michael Dixon and Liz Engelman.

SCENE 1

The Miles residence. The living room. At rise, we see a couch with plush pillows. An Elmo doll sits on the couch. KAREN MILES, in a rush, is running around, wearing a business suit, one earring and one shoe. Even at her frenetic pace, and late for a meeting, she maintains a sense of humor about it all. In a singsong, cooing voice, KAREN calls out to her young child, LAILA (pronounced "Lay-lah").

KAREN: Laila, I only have one shoe, isn't that silly?! Laila? Have you seen my other shoe?

There is no answer. KAREN finds the shoe. She calls out again, throwing her voice toward the offstage area.

KAREN: I found it, sweetie.

There is no answer. She glances offstage to try to spot her child.

KAREN: Sweetie, can you hear me? Laila! Have you seen my other earring?

There is no answer. KAREN finds her earring on an Elmo doll. She calls out, playful:

KAREN: Laila, is there a reason Elmo is wearing my earring? Does Elmo have a meeting right now? Come give mommy a hug, sweetie! Sweetie?

As she looks offstage for Laila, KAREN picks up a fringed silk scarf and starts draping it around herself. The doorbell rings. She rushes to open the door.

LAURIE: Hi, Mrs. Miles? I'm Laurie.

KAREN: *(rapid-fire)* Laurie! Thank God you came over so quickly. It's really an emergency. It's very nice to meet you. You come very highly recommended by the Morrissons, Cathy, and the Olson boy . . .

LAURIE: Mike? *(smiles)* I taught him everything he knows about babysitting. And algebra. And a few other things.

KAREN: I used to feel very strongly about rigorous screening for all babysitters. And David generally insists on questioning sitters for at least 90 minutes on the phone and then in person but he's away and you—seem fine.

LAURIE: You can ask me anything.

KAREN: Um. How old are you?

LAURIE: Seventeen.

KAREN: *(quickly)* Good age. So. I have a meeting. Don't know how late it will go. But while I'm gone, here is a list of things you might like to do with Laila. Though I should warn you no babysitter has ever gotten her to do any item on this list. You can feed her anything in the fridge, but her favorite foods are pot roast, dry toast, and dry cereal. She can play in the yard as long as you watch her. Good night!

LAURIE: Mrs. Miles? Where is Laila?

KAREN: Oh right. *(Calling to offstage child)* Laila!

KAREN looks stage left. LAURIE looks in the same direction. Then KAREN suddenly turns her head stage right as if she is watching somebody run. As she jerks her head to the right, there is a whooshing sound heard.

KAREN: There she goes. She is so fast! She's got so much energy that sometimes you can hardly see her. Watch her go.

KAREN and LAURIE both look offstage right; then, in sync, their heads whoosh to stage left. They're like the audience of a ping-pong match.

LAURIE: Wow. Laila . . .

KAREN: I know. I know. She's a blur.

LAURIE *(Smiles as "LAILA" whooshes by again)* I remember being a blur. *(Another whoosh.)*

KAREN: Do you really? Whoosh, there she goes again. If you can ever get her to sit in one place, try the list. See you soon!

KAREN exits. LAURIE addresses the empty space where she believes LAILA is.

LAURIE: Hi Laila! My name is Laurie. I'm your new babysitter.

A whooshing sound as the blurring child goes by. LAURIE turns in the other direction, nervous.

LAURIE: So. Um. I think you're over there now. You have a lot of energy Laila, that's great. Like I said, I'm Laurie. You're Laila. We both have L's in our names! Do you know a lot of my closest friends start with L? It's a

great letter. Do you know about the letter L? It starts a lot of words. Like
La. La la la!!!

LAURIE waits. No response.

LAURIE: Laila do you like jacks? I brought jacks.

LAILA whooshes by and LAURIE turns again.

LAURIE: Laila, would you like to eat a pot roast sandwich on dry toast in
the shape of an L? You know, your favorite foods get better when you try
them in a new shape.

*The sound of a child's footsteps is heard. LAURIE looks offstage in the
direction of the sound, which comes from a "doorway" that is just beyond
the edge of the stage and hovering above the audience. LAURIE sees "LAILA"
in the threshold of the doorway.*

LAURIE: There you are! You like shapes?

A silence. LAURIE reacts as "LAILA" nods.

LAURIE: Let's go!

*Whoosh sound as "LAILA," invisible to the audience, and LAURIE both run
blurry fast into the kitchen; then whoosh morphs into rock music as lights
fade out.*

SCENE 2

Lights up two hours later, sounds of a violin playing. KAREN enters.

KAREN: Laurie! I'm home. Laurie? Where are you? Where's Laila?

*LAURIE enters through the screen door and points out the window, where
LAILA sits practicing her violin in the yard.*

LAURIE: She's right there. Practicing violin.

KAREN: What? Oh my god. I thought that was the radio. Laila sometimes
turns on W-H-O-A. *(confesses)* I've never actually heard her play before!

LAURIE: You haven't?

The music is fading out by now, becoming soft and then inaudible. During the following, music should waft in occasionally to suggest more continuous playing, rather than underscoring the whole scene.

KAREN: *(shakes her head)* She learned in school. What did you say to get her to practice? Did you offer her a toy? Money?

LAURIE: I told her music is more fun outdoors, so she wanted to try it.

KAREN: *(suspicious)* How do you know what's fun?

LAURIE: *(figuring this out as she says it)* I don't. I just guess. I try to sense it.

KAREN: *(disgusted)* Sense it. Sense it. Okay . . . I see practicing outdoors could have a certain—*(suddenly this hits her)* Practicing outdoors! My goodness. There are noise ordinances in Westchester. What about the neighbors? Didn't anyone complain?

LAURIE: Which neighbors?

KAREN: The Grotzes.

LAURIE: Don't know any Grotzes. Didn't hear from them.

KAREN: Excellent.

LAURIE: *(suddenly remembering)* There was this guy Alvin—

KAREN: That's him! Alvin Grotz!

LAURIE: Oh, I didn't get his last name. Yeah, he did come over.

KAREN: *(horrified)* And?

LAURIE: He's still here. See? *(pointing out the window)* He brought his clarinet. They've been improvising.

KAREN: Alvin Grotz plays the clarinet?

LAURIE: Yeah, they've been jamming! And I brought my flute! So we did Bach's Violin Concerto #2 in E Major. You know . . .

She starts humming a melody from the concerto.

KAREN: You're a musician?

LAURIE: No, I suck. But Bach, he's good. And Alvin, he's good too. There, he just came in.

Sounds of violin and clarinet can be heard together.

LAURIE: And his wife, Shelly? She plays cello.

KAREN: Shelly Grotz plays cello?

LAURIE: She has a master's degree in music. Shelly couldn't tonight but she wants to come to the next rehearsal.

KAREN: There's a next rehearsal?

LAURIE: Not officially. Just a general sense that there should be music in the moonlight.

KAREN: I see.

LAURIE: But Laila said Tuesdays would be best for her.

KAREN: She did? Did she . . . eat any dinner? I should've warned you she doesn't eat much. My husband says she once finished a peach but I wasn't here.

LAURIE: *(not bragging, just trying to remember dinner)* She had pot roast with toast, a side salad, a carrot, a few pieces of cereal, and a medallion of cold poached salmon. Then she had dessert.

KAREN: She did? How did you do that?

LAURIE: I just used the promise of dessert. I told her if she tried enough of the other foods, she could finish with a popcorn sandwich using mini-chocolate bars as bread. You know, two little chocolates, three pieces of popcorn.

KAREN: What made you think this would work?

LAURIE: Haven't you ever been to the movies and dropped chocolate into your popcorn?

KAREN: No.

LAURIE: It works.

KAREN: It does sound good. I'm going to make some cocoa. Would you like some cocoa?

LAURIE: Sure.

(KAREN gets up to heat the cocoa. On her way back she looks out the window.) I also put the dry cereal pieces into her salad. For kids her age, Cheerios are like croutons.

KAREN: Did you just make that up or is that a verified fact?

LAURIE *(not sure)* I think everything I know about babysitting is a made-up verified fact?

KAREN: *(looks out the window and calls to Laila)* That's very beautiful, darling! *(to Laurie)* Don't you think she plays rather remarkably well?

LAURIE: Yes.

KAREN: Did you—play that well, as a child?

LAURIE: I don't play that well now.

KAREN nods, takes this in.)

KAREN: Did she ask you where I was?

LAURIE: It . . . didn't come up.

KAREN: Why is that, do you think?

LAURIE: I probably just distracted her.

KAREN: Right. *(KAREN brings out the cocoa in red mugs and serves it, a little apprehensive)* Was anything else . . . accomplished?

LAURIE: Let's see. She did her alphabet homework, dressed Elmo in a necktie, glued her broken china doll together, took a bath, finished putting the photos in her album, braided her hair . . .

KAREN: Are you mocking me?

LAURIE: Mocking you, Mrs. Miles?

KAREN: After I told you no one could do anything on the list—to go and do the whole list like that—

LAURIE: Did we? I stopped using the list.

KAREN: What?

LAURIE: Laila . . . reminded me of that blur time. When I liked things to be sudden and surprising. So I thought I'd do better without the list. Don't you remember it?

KAREN: Remember what?

LAURIE: Childhood.

KAREN: God, no.

LAURIE: I forget more every day. But I try to remember it when I'm with children.

KAREN: I not only can't remember . . . I don't even know where to start.

She starts sniffling, almost crying.

LAURIE: Oh Mrs. Miles.

KAREN: And then—you come in here and show me what a complete failure I am!

LAURIE: I'm sorry.

KAREN: Get out of my house!

LAURIE: I can't do that. (*The violin music changes to Mozart.*)

KAREN: Oh, you think you can stay and help me? You can't. David and I—have no idea what we're doing. We've read all the books you're supposed to read, the one by the big college professor with the beard, and the one by the guru about what drives the human soul, and the one by the priestess woman with the necklaces, and not one of these books explain our daughter one little bit. Half the time, we don't even know where she is, she runs so fast. And now she's—playing Mozart! (*starts crying again*) So you can leave. You can't help. But you can leave.

LAURIE: I can't leave because you owe me money.

KAREN: Oh, so it's all about money, you don't give a shit about Laila!

LAURIE: I didn't say that, Mrs. Miles!

KAREN: How much do I owe you, kid?

LAURIE: Six to 8:30 is two and a half hours. I charge ten an hour. So you owe me $25.

KAREN: Oh my god. You did all that in two and a half hours?

LAURIE: It's very common, Mrs. Miles, for a child to behave differently with a babysitter than with her parents.

KAREN: Yes, but it's not as common for a hyperactive little blur to suddenly turn into Itzhak Perlman!

LAURIE: That's less common.

KAREN: Here's your money.

LAURIE: Thanks. So I should be going.

KAREN: Good night.

The music stops. LAURIE gets up. Suddenly KAREN turns to her.

KAREN: Laurie! Laurie. I can't remember any of it . . . Can you show me how? Remind me?

LAURIE: *(sits back down)* No. But you can feel it. You're in it now.

KAREN: What?

LAURIE: You're sinking into the couch, Mrs. Miles. Surrounded by plush pillows. And you're wearing a soft silky scarf with fringe. Drinking hot cocoa with mini-marshmallows from a square red mug with a rounded handle. And in some of the sips of cocoa, you get two or three mini-marshmallows! This is it.

KAREN: It is? Now? Just now this is it?

LAURIE: No, not yet. Just at that moment when you sip the cocoa and stop talking about it.

They sip in silence. The music starts again, a beautiful melody. A stunning flourish on the violin. Followed by quiet. Blissful, both women settle into the sofa beside the Elmo doll. KAREN takes a deep breath and giggles. LAURIE giggles too. KAREN pulls off an earring and puts it on the doll. She slips off her shoes. Then she takes another sip of cocoa.

KAREN: Mmmmmm.

CURTAIN

Discussion on Writing *The Popcorn Sonata*

by Jenny Lyn Bader

I wrote *The Popcorn Sonata* in 2002, when the Off-Broadway theater company Primary Stages invited a number of playwrights to contribute short plays to a theme-based evening. It was just a few months after 9/11. The event was too raw to write about, yet it seemed in its wake difficult to write about anything else. So the chosen theme was "A Moment of Bliss." The idea was, amid a pervasive feeling of tragedy, to find a small pocket of hope. Where, in those dark days, might one find a hint of joy—even if it lasted only briefly? Each play, whether light or dark, needed to feature just that.

This idea of a "moment of bliss" reminded me of Virginia Woolf's quest for "moments of being," the modernist desire for glimpses of heightened vision, special connection, and intense awareness in a world lacking intimacy and permanence. As Woolf writes in *To the Lighthouse*,

> What is the meaning of life? The great revelation had never come. The great revelation perhaps never did come. Instead there were little daily miracles, illuminations, matches struck unexpectedly in the dark.

Woolf reminds us in her essay collection *Moments of Being* that "a great part of every day is not lived consciously." Those bits of time when one becomes conscious of being, then, become the transcendent moments that make life worth living. Ideally a moment of bliss should also be transcendent, though it occurred to me that rather than being self-aware, it might instead be strikingly free of consciousness.

Considering the idea of pure bliss, I decided I wanted to write about the bliss of childhood, the feeling of uncontained exuberance that we so often forget when we grow up. Wondering how to express that onstage, I concluded that the theatrical device I needed was an invisible child—one who runs so fast, has so much energy, and is so caught up in the delight of childhood that it's hard to see her. Sometimes she appears to be invisible. When seen, she frequently looks like a "blur" to adults, including her own mother. Then I would introduce a babysitter character who would be younger, closer to childhood than the mother. The sitter would have the challenge of locating said blissful child and would need to figure out some way to catch a glimpse of her.

How to make the invisible seen onstage? One way was through the visible characters watching the frenetic, joyous blur run by. Another way was through music, which I incorporated into the play.

Somehow it was not until I had finished the first draft of the play that I realized it was the second play I had written involving invisible characters, and that it might be a companion piece to my short play *The Third First Blind Double Date*. I then began thinking about whether I might have yet another play to complete a full-length evening . . . though I didn't figure out what that would be for a while.

I have found that the perspectives of other writers can always be valu-able in play development, even for a short piece. During my time as a Lark playwriting fellow, I brought this piece into the playwrights' workshop there. In particular, I was trying to define the moment where the child set-tles down and is briefly "seen," and refine the stage direction there, using lights, or perhaps a pair of shoes peeking in from just offstage . . . Tina Howe encouraged me to add a stage direction where we hear the footsteps of the child but still don't see her feet. Not every director has followed that direction, of course, but when it can be pulled off, I think it is a highly sat-isfying, theatrical moment. That stage direction also ensures that no one tries to cast the offstage child, which would not be as effective a way of celebrating the joy and poetry of childhood. In that same workshop ses-sion, Arthur Kopit asked about David, the offstage husband. As I revised the play, I looked at it from each character's point of view, as I always do. Then, inspired by Arthur's question, I also considered the viewpoints of the offstage characters and added just a little more detail about them, for instance: "My husband said she once finished a peach but I wasn't here."

Eventually I decided to write an entire play cycle contemplating invis-ibility, where in each playlet, there is someone who goes unseen in a differ-ent way. That decision led to another revision as I wanted the plays to be connected not only by theme but also by recurring characters. I went back over all of them, incorporating characters I invented later into plays writ-ten earlier. So when Karen says, "We've read all the books you're supposed to read, the one by the big college professor with the beard, and the one by the guru about what drives the human soul, and the one by the priestess woman with the necklaces"—she is referring to characters in some of the other plays in *Out of Mind: 7 Short Plays with Some of the People Missing*. Of course, if someone asked my permission, I would allow them to cut that line if they were performing just *Popcorn Sonata* without the others and needed to cut something for time, but even out of context the line makes sense . . . and offers more detail about the offstage husband, too.

One thing I discovered in auditions and rehearsals for some of these productions and readings was that for the play to work, the babysitter has to be in a state of discovery and wonder, too, rather than a know-it-all—a natural and an innocent rather than smug or superior. While she does calm the mother, she also has to be a bit nervous herself at times. That way, both characters have the opportunity to grow. Before the play was first pub-lished, I added a couple of stage directions to clarify some of the charac-ter questions that came up in rehearsal. And I added a few technical stage directions, too, as I learned about the play in production. In particular I noted when the music should stop playing, because I realized that even though the play is deeply based in music, too much underscoring can be detrimental to it.

Ultimately, it is the unseen, unheard child who has the last word here. I should add that when I wrote *The Popcorn Sonata*—and when I completed the rest of the "invisible plays" on the themes of seeing others and being seen, I did not yet have children. But then I did have children, which caused me to look at those plays in a new way. When my daughter was four, she went to a birthday party at a gym and refused to enter the gym but watched from a hallway window. When asked why she had not gone inside to play with the other children she said, "I was worried they would notice me . . . and they would think that I wasn't there." She hadn't seen the plays. She didn't have to. As a child, she intuitively knew more about the fear of invisibility than I did—and about its wonder.

On the Edge

by Craig Pospisil

It is night, and GENE, a young man of 17, stands on a ledge on the outside of a New York City building, ten stories up in the air. He is plastered to the wall and is very careful with any movement. He forces himself to look down at the street and scans it for a few seconds before looking up again.

Several feet away from him there is a dimly lit, open window. From inside the apartment low levels of rock music and snatches of conversation from a party can sometimes be heard.

After a few moments, SAMMY, a young woman of 17, appears in the window. Gene freezes, hoping not to be seen by her. Sammy sticks an unlit cigarette in her mouth and pulls a match out of a matchbook. She strikes the match against the book a couple of times, but it won't light. She tosses the match out the window . . . and notices Gene.

Long pause. They look at one another.

SAMMY: Hey.

GENE: Hey.

Sammy glances down at the sidewalk below as she tears another match from the book and tries lighting it. Before it catches, though, Gene speaks up.

GENE: Ah . . . would you mind waiting a couple minutes?

SAMMY: Hm?

GENE: Cigarette smoke really bothers me.

SAMMY: Oh. Sure.

Gene looks down and scans the sidewalk again. Sammy watches him.

SAMMY: So, what's up? You're missing the party.

GENE: I'm just hanging out.

SAMMY: That's cool. *(Pause)* How's the view?

GENE: I can see my building from here.

SAMMY: *(Slight pause)* I know you. You're in my physics class, right?

GENE: Yeah.

SAMMY: What's your name?

GENE: Gene.

SAMMY: Right. Right.

GENE: You're Samantha. Sammy.

SAMMY: Yeah. How'd you know?

GENE: . . . you're in my physics class.

SAMMY: Oh. Yeah. *(Pause)* So, what're you doing?

GENE: What does it look like I'm doing?

SAMMY: It looks like a major bid for attention.

GENE: With *my* parents? I stopped trying.

SAMMY: *(pause)* So, what's the deal?

GENE: *(shrugs)* I decided life's just not worth it.

SAMMY: Bummer. *(pause)* So, what're you waiting for?

GENE: Amanda.

SAMMY: Amanda Harris?

Gene nods. Sammy looks over her shoulder into the apartment and then back at Gene.

SAMMY: You want me to get her?

GENE: No, I'm waiting for her to leave.

SAMMY: But then you'll miss her.

GENE: Not by much.

SAMMY: Whoa. That's harsh.

GENE: Yeah, well . . . so's life.

SAMMY: So, what happened? She dump you?

GENE: We weren't dating.

SAMMY: So, she wouldn't go out with you.

GENE: . . . uh, not really.

SAMMY: *(slight pause)* Did you ask her out? *(pause)* Gene?

GENE: I don't wanna talk about it.

SAMMY: Hey, I just want to be able to tell people why you did it. I mean, I'm sure to be interviewed by the news and the tabloids. After they hose you off the sidewalk.

GENE: They'll know.

SAMMY: Did you leave a note?

GENE: *(slight pause)* No.

SAMMY: Do you want some paper?

GENE: Would you go away?

SAMMY: If you don't leave a note, how's anyone gonna know why you did it?

GENE: Because I'm gonna scream her name out as I fall, okay?!

SAMMY: *(pause)* What if you can't finish?

GENE: What?

SAMMY: I mean, do you have this timed out? How long will it take? Probably the sort of thing I could figure out if I paid attention during physics. But, I mean, what if you only get to say, "Aman—!" before you hit?

GENE: I'll finish.

SAMMY: There's a breeze. What if the wind takes the sound away?

GENE: I'll make sure they hear me.

SAMMY: I'm just trying to help.

GENE: I think I can handle it. *(pause)* You know, this isn't gonna be pretty. I'm gonna split open on the sidewalk when I hit. If I don't jump far enough, I might impale myself on that iron fencing. So, unless you wanna have nightmares about this for the rest of your life, you might wanna go.

SAMMY: No, I'm cool. *(pause)* I don't think Amanda knows you like her so much.

GENE: I don't like her. I *love* her.

SAMMY: Whatever. You should tell her.

GENE: *(pause)* I can't.

SAMMY: It's gotta be easier than this.

GENE: Yeah, but this makes more of statement.

SAMMY: A statement about what?

GENE: It's just more dramatic, okay?!

SAMMY: Oh! I know where else I've seen you. You're in all the plays at school, right?

GENE: Yeah.

SAMMY: No wonder.

GENE: "No wonder" what?

SAMMY: You theater people are weird.

GENE: We are not!

SAMMY: Dude, you're on a ledge.

GENE: You don't understand.

SAMMY: Maybe not. *(slight pause)* Does your shrink understand?

GENE: I don't go to a shrink!

SAMMY: Something to think about. *(slight pause)* But, you know, Amanda's not so great. She's got a hot body, yeah, but she's kinda obvious. I mean, she's the sort of pretty you like to look at, but I can't imagine what I'd talk to her about.

GENE: No, she's really nice. She always smiles at me in the halls at school, and sometimes I run into her when I'm walking my dog, and we say hi, and then she talks to Molly and pets her. She's not like you think. *(slight pause)* I love her voice. It's kind of rough, but sweet.

SAMMY: Yeah, she's got a kinda sexy voice. *(pause)* So, where do you live?

GENE: What?

SAMMY: I live near Amanda, too. East 78th between Park and Lex. Where are you?

GENE: Why do you want to know?

SAMMY: Jeez, I'm just curious. I thought maybe we could share a cab across the park.

GENE: After I kill myself?!

SAMMY: Oh, yeah, right. I forgot.

GENE: Stick around. You'll see.

SAMMY: Uh-huh. *(pause)* Wait a minute. You said you could see your building. This is the West Side. You don't live near Amanda.

GENE: *(slight pause)* I didn't say I did. I said I saw her walking my dog.

SAMMY: Oh, man.

GENE: What?

SAMMY: Tell me you don't drag your dog across town, hoping you'll run into her.

GENE: No. We just go for long walks.

SAMMY: Oh, man! You're like a stalker.

GENE: I am not.

SAMMY: Oh, wow. Now that's an angle for the tabloids. Wait 'til I tell people.

GENE: No! Don't! *(slight pause)* Please.

SAMMY: Then come back inside and talk to her.

GENE: No. I can't.

SAMMY: Why not? I'll help you find—*[her.]*

GENE: *(interrupting)* Because she's got her tongue halfway down Bobby Chamberlain's throat, okay?!! *(pause)* I ran into her when I was walking

Molly last weekend, and we talked and she said she was coming to M.J.'s party tonight, and I said I was too, and she said, "Great. I'll see you there. We can hang out." I've been waiting all week for this party. I thought, "Perfect. We'll talk a little and then I'll ask her out." I've wanted to for months, but first she was dating Dean and then Chris, but . . . . Well, I got here right at eight. I was the first one here. And I waited near the door. And I waited. And waited. And I drank a lot while I was waiting, . . . and then she came in. And Bobby had his arm around her neck. *(pause)* So, then I had to go throw up for a while. And when I got back she was making out with him on the couch. So then I went to throw up a little more, and as I came out of the bathroom, I saw them duck into M.J.'s mother's bedroom. *(slight pause)* All I wanted was to hold her hand and smell her hair, and she's down the hall fucking him!

Long pause.

SAMMY: Bobby's kinda cute, you know.

GENE: What?!

SAMMY: Well, he is.

GENE: He's an idiot. We've been going to school together for six years and he still can't remember my name. He's always . . . I mean, it's like other people just don't . . . . He's an asshole!

SAMMY: Hey, he's not my type, but a lot of girls go for him.

GENE: Oh, go away! Please?!

SAMMY: The thing is you shouldn't have waited to ask her.

GENE: Like I don't know that! Like that's not the reason I'm out here. I'm a loser. I'm weak! No one wants to be around me. I get it! I know, okay?! *(slight pause)* I can't take it any more, all right?! I'm tired. I'm tired of trying to "just keep smiling," like my mother says. Or go, "Well, some people are late bloomers." *(pause)* I can't.

Long pause

SAMMY: Gene . . .

GENE: What?

SAMMY: I've got bad news.

GENE: You're fucked up, you know that!

SAMMY: Amanda's gone.

GENE: *(slight pause)* Bullshit. I'm not falling for that.

SAMMY: You must've missed her while we were talking. I bummed that cigarette from her as she and Bobby left.

GENE: No! You're lying! I've been watching. I couldn't have missed her.

SAMMY: Okay, fine. Keep waiting then. I'm going back inside.

GENE: No, wait!

SAMMY: What?

GENE: You're just gonna go in there and tell people or call the cops. Or you'll tell Amanda not to leave.

SAMMY: I'm telling you, Gene, she's already gone.

GENE: I was watching.

SAMMY: Fine, she's still here. Me, I need a drink.

GENE: If you go, I'll jump.

SAMMY: Yeah, so? I thought you were gonna jump anyway.

GENE: But I'll jump now. And it'll be your fault.

SAMMY: I can live with that.

Sammy turns and disappears into the apartment.

GENE: Hey! Sammy? Sammy?! *(slight pause)* Bitch!

Sammy suddenly reappears in the window.

SAMMY: Wha'd you call me?!

Gene flinches and struggles to keep his balance.

GENE: Jesus Christ! Don't do that.

SAMMY: What did you call me?

GENE: Oh, give me a break.

SAMMY: No one calls me that!

GENE: Everyone calls you that!

SAMMY: What?

GENE: Everyone calls you a bitch. *(slight pause)* And after tonight I know why!

SAMMY: Knock it off, asshole!

GENE: Or what?

Sammy climbs out onto the ledge and starts inching her way toward Gene.

GENE: What the hell are you doing?!

SAMMY: I'm gonna make you shut up.

GENE: You stay away! You . . . oh, I get it. This is like reverse psychology, right? You say you're gonna push me, so I say, "No, no, I want to live."

SAMMY: No, I'm just pushing you.

GENE: I'll take you with me!

SAMMY: Like I care.

GENE: Okay-I'm-sorry-I'm-sorry. I'm sorry.

Sammy stops. She is about a foot or so away from him.

SAMMY: Fine, whatever. Forget it. *(She looks around for the first time.)* Hey . . . this is kinda cool out here.

There is a pause as Gene gets his breath back.

GENE: Oh, man, I am so fucked up.

SAMMY: You just need to talk to a shrink or something.

GENE: I don't think I could.

SAMMY: It's not so hard.

GENE: *(slight pause)* You go to one?

SAMMY: Yeah.

GENE: How come?

SAMMY: My parents make me go.

GENE: You're kidding. Why?

SAMMY: They're worried I'm a lesbian.

GENE: Oh, that's fucked! Why do they think that?

SAMMY: 'Cause I'm a lesbian.

GENE: *(pause)* What?

SAMMY: I like girls.

GENE: Really?

SAMMY: Yeah.

GENE: Whoa. *(slight pause)* What's that like?

SAMMY: I don't know. Probably like you liking girls.

GENE: Does anyone else know?

SAMMY: *(slight pause)* No.

GENE: What does your shrink say?

SAMMY: Not much.

GENE: What do you say?

SAMMY: That I don't have a problem liking girls.

GENE: Is that true?

SAMMY: Yeah. I mean, it's . . . . No. I don't have a problem with it. My folks are kinda messed up about the idea, though. They said they'd like disown me or not pay for college or something. It's a drag.

GENE: So, what are you going to do?

SAMMY: I don't know. Try to hold out until I get through school and college and then get away or something.

GENE: That sucks.

SAMMY: I guess.

They are silent for a moment.

GENE: My parents are nuts, but . . . not like that.

SAMMY: Good.

GENE: You wanna go back in?

SAMMY: In a minute. It's kinda fun out here.

GENE: Yeah, it's a rush when the wind blows by.

SAMMY: Yeah?

GENE: Yeah. Wait . . . here it comes.

They stand there feeling the breeze. As the wind picks up, they spread their arms flat against the wall for extra support. Their hands touch, and Gene and Sammy look at each other. Smiling, they take each other's hand and feel the wind blowing by.

THE LIGHTS FADE TO BLACK.

END OF PLAY

Creating *On the Edge*

by Craig Pospisil

I wrote *On the Edge* a number of years ago after going through a divorce. During the divorce proceedings it occurred to me that some of the emotions I was having were every bit as dramatic (and melodramatic) as feelings I'd had when I was a teenager desperately in love with a girl, who didn't feel that way about me. I decided to write about what I was going through in the present (the divorce), but to approach it through the guise of a seventeen year-old kid. Seventeen was the age I was, but I thought it worked well too because it's an age that stands at the end of what is considered—legally at least—childhood and the beginning of adulthood. I also remember that year as a time of enormous drama for my friends and me. We felt everything so keenly, and yet we also were often putting on an air of cynical detachment: so jaded, we'd seen it all.

I like to play with opposition when I write. I like to take a set of circumstances that look or sound familiar and then subvert that, and play against the audience's expectations. That isn't to say that I throw in a sharp right turn without warning or justification, but I like to defy expectations as a way of revealing something about my characters. The unexpected can also be a great source of comedy, which is what I usually write and what this play is.

I tend to use elements from my own life when I'm writing. So in thinking about what to write, the first character to come to mind was a variation on my younger self. Gene is a bit shy, still trying to figure out who he is and how he fits into the world. He's full of big emotions, but doesn't know how to express them. He's also an actor, so he also has a flair for the dramatic and grand gestures. One of the big dramatic events of my senior year in high school was a disastrous cast party after a play we'd done. The guy throwing the party hadn't told his parents, who were out that night, and the party got out of hand, with a lot of freshmen showing up uninvited, and then drinking too much and making out in corners. In the middle of this scene, one of my best friends learned that everyone in the class knew that he was gay. He was very upset to find himself outed this way, and several of us had to leave the party to talk things out with him. In my mind, that's the party Gene is at. Even though the audience will never know about that party and the rest, it helps make the piece all the more specific and real to me.

On the Edge begins with Gene literally on the edge. He's standing on a ledge on the tenth floor of a building, threatening to jump because a girl he's madly in love with is making out with some other guy. (For the record, in real life, no one went out on a window ledge at that party. But to my mind that was the kind of oh-so-dramatic thing a teenager might consider.) This starts the play with pretty high stakes right away. And just inside the window next to him, the audience can hear the sounds of a party—rock music play, people laughing—so that is also in opposition to Gene's situation. While Gene is standing there, a girl, Sammy, who's a classmate of Gene's, comes to the window to smoke a cigarette. The expectation is built in that Sammy will try to talk Gene off the ledge and back into the apartment. Someone's life is in danger, so the audience's assumption will be that the play is about getting that person out of danger.

To work against that I wrote Sammy like she didn't care. If Gene has all the over-wrought, deeply felt emotions of a teenager, Sammy has all of the "yeah, whatever" and jaded attitude of teenagers. As I started to write Sammy I decided that not only would she not try to talk Gene off the ledge, but in fact she makes fun of him for being so dramatic, teases him, basically dares him to jump.

Sammy continues to tease him and in doing so pulls some details from Gene about why he's on the ledge. This drives the play from the initial meeting into the next phase where the two of them start to be more honest with each other and reveal things about themselves. Sammy starts to understand that Gene isn't just being melodramatic, but he's in a very bad place. But by then she's pushed Gene away so far that he doesn't believe her when she genuinely tries to help him, and he responds very angrily.

When I first started *On the Edge*, I wasn't sure exactly where the story was going to go or how it would end. But I did know two things that I did *not* want to do. First of all, I didn't want Gene and Sammy to end up as a couple. He wears his heart on his sleeve, she's the tough girl who saves his life, they find love. I felt that would be too obvious, and it wouldn't really be realistic. I wanted to make Gene and Sammy a pair of lonely kids, misfits, who make a connection to one another. Which, I think, is hard enough to do in this world.

That was one of the reasons I decided to make Sammy a lesbian. It removed the possibility of a love relationship between her and Gene. Her sexuality wasn't something I planned from the start. In fact, it only occurred to me at the point in the play where she announces it to Gene. But I'd happened to write a line for her in which she talked about going to therapy and another where she commented that Amanda, the girl Gene loves, has a "sexy voice." Those were instances of simply trying to write a "worldly" character that ended up supporting the choice for her sexuality. But I also loved what the revelation of her sexuality did for her character. Gene had been the one whose life we learned about through the piece as he talked about Amanda and about his parents, whereas Sammy had been quiet about herself. The way she reveals herself to Gene and what she tells him after that makes her a much more human character.

The second thing I knew I did *not* want to do in the play was connected to the ending. When I began writing it, I didn't know how it would end, but I knew how I didn't want it to end. At first there seemed to be two ways the story could end: with Gene coming in off the ledge, or with him jumping to his death. The play is a comedy, so he couldn't really jump without the play taking a very dark turn. But that made the idea of him going back inside too obvious, the expected choice.

So I decided that I had to leave him on the outside of the building for some reason. But if he wasn't coming in, what would keep him out there? So I built up the argument between Gene and Sammy to the point where Sammy goes out on the ledge, too. In fact, she's threatening to push him off, putting both of them in danger. Once the argument that propelled Sammy out on the ledge is over, it leaves both of them in a very exposed place—emotionally and physically—and that allows them to make a very real connection to each other. And at that point, it seemed perfect to leave them there, almost savoring the danger, on the edge of their own coming adulthood and lives.

The Pain in the Poetry

by Glenn Alterman

CAST:

SHERIDAN: He may seem timid, but has inner passion and power.

PAMELA: Sheridan's wife. She may seem cool, controlling, but also has warmth and deep passion.

NOTE: Both SHERIDAN and PAMELA can be played by actors as young as their thirties or as old as their fifties or sixties. They must be believable as a married couple.

THE SET: There is no set.

PAMELA is seated in a comfortable chair (possibly a rocking chair), knitting. Next to her chair is a large knitting basket. SHERIDAN enters, stands in front of her.

SHERIDAN: *(Meekly, softly)* I wrote a play.

PAMELA: *(Looking up)* Hm, what?

SHERIDAN: *(A little bolder)* I said, I wrote a play.

PAMELA: That's nice, dear. Did you feed the dog?

SHERIDAN: Did you hear what I said?

PAMELA: Yes, you said you wrote a play or something.

SHERIDAN: A full-length!

PAMELA: And I asked you if you fed the dog.

SHERIDAN: One act with no intermission.

PAMELA: The dog hasn't eaten all day.

SHERIDAN: *(Blurting it out)* It's been my whole life for the last two years!

PAMELA: What has, your play?

SHERIDAN: Every second at work when I wasn't working I was working on it!

PAMELA: You were?

SHERIDAN: On lunch hours, in subway stations, on stairwells! Anywhere, anytime, whenever I had a moment it was just me . . .

PAMELA: I see.

SHERIDAN: . . . alone with my play!

PAMELA: Why didn't you tell me?

SHERIDAN: I couldn't.

PAMELA: Why not?

SHERIDAN: It was—too private. Something I had to do alone; something I couldn't share with anyone.

PAMELA: Not even me.

SHERIDAN: *(An edge)* Especially not you.

PAMELA: I see.

SHERIDAN: Then late last night, well actually early this morning, while you were asleep, I finished it, on the bathroom floor, by candlelight.

PAMELA: I wondered why you were spending so much time in there.

SHERIDAN: I didn't want to talk about it until it was all down on paper. I was afraid.

PAMELA: Of what?

SHERIDAN: Giving away the ending.

PAMELA: But you say it's over now?

SHERIDAN: Yes. Finished. Complete. Done.

PAMELA: *(SHE puts her knitting down. Gently, sincerely.)* Well, I'm glad you told me. I understand.

SHERIDAN: Do you?

PAMELA: Yes. Now let's just forget about it and go on as if . . . *(Suddenly SHERIDAN walks away from her)* Where are you going, what's wrong?

SHERIDAN: Nothing.

PAMELA: Tell me. *(HE stops, looks guiltily at her.)* There isn't another one, is there?

SHERIDAN: No.

PAMELA: Don't lie to me!

SHERIDAN: I tell you I haven't written another word!

PAMELA: I won't put up with it; the bathroom, backstreets, another two years!

SHERIDAN: I said, I haven't-written-a-word!

PAMELA: Okay, all right.

SHERIDAN: But . . .

PAMELA: What?

SHERIDAN: I've been having these "thoughts."

PAMELA: What kind of thoughts?

SHERIDAN: *(Filled with guilt)* Snippets, little snippets—of dialogue.

PAMELA: No!

SHERIDAN: *(Walking away, tormented)* Yes, this two-character scene keeps playing over and over in my head. All right, I admit it, YES, I'm thinking about another play!

PAMELA: You can't be! You just finished one, this morning. My God, what kind of insatiable . . . ?!

SHERIDAN: I was lying there on the bathroom floor, satisfied, content. Holding my play lovingly in my arms. Caressing it, fingering the folder. When I heard the faucet drip.

PAMELA: The faucet?

SHERIDAN: Drip, drip-drop; a lovely sound, really.

PAMELA: You were holding your play in . . . ? Caressing it?!

SHERIDAN: I gently put it down by my side, and just listened to the water for a while. Drip, drip-drop, drip-drop. Sounded like, I don't know, little feet.

PAMELA: Little feet?

SHERIDAN: Tiny, little, tap-dancing feet. I lay there on the floor for I don't know how long, just listening. When suddenly it hit me!

PAMELA: What, the water?

SHERIDAN: No, the thought.

PAMELA: What thought?

SHERIDAN: Maybe . . . maybe a musical!

PAMELA: A musical?!

SHERIDAN: You know, dancing, singing . . .

PAMELA: We are a family, have you forgotten?!

SHERIDAN: *(Walking away)* Don't.

PAMELA: You have a job, responsibilities. And what about me, huh, us?!

SHERIDAN: *(Stopping)* I'm sorry, it's just something I have to do!

PAMELA: *(Getting worked up)* What's next, huh?! A comedy, some cheap comedy? Oh I can just see it now, you and your dirty little comedy. The two of you having lots of laughs in some dark stairwell together. A chuckle on the bathroom floor. Dirty jokes, pathetic puns. Well I'm telling you right now your fun's over. I will not play second fiddle to some musical!

SHE gathers her knitting, starts to leave.

SHERIDAN: Where you going?

PAMELA: I'm leaving you—playwright!

SHERIDAN: *(HE grabs her arm)* Don't leave, please! *(As she pulls her arm free, her knitting basket accidentally opens up. Hundreds of sheets of paper fall out. They both stop, see the papers fall.)* What are those?

PAMELA: *(Quickly gathering some of the papers)* Nothing, knitting instructions.

SHERIDAN: *(Picking one up, reading it)* This is your handwriting.

PAMELA: *(Trying to grab it from him)* Give me that!

SHERIDAN: What is this?

PAMELA: Scribblings, recipes. Give me that paper!

SHERIDAN: It's . . . it's a poem! *(Looking at her, astonished)* You've been writing poetry.

PAMELA: Yes, all right, I had to do something! What was I supposed to do, knit all day?! You were always away, or upstairs locked in the bathroom.

I was going out of my mind with loneliness. Then one day in my despair, a couplet came to me. A rhyme, and then a verse. A beautiful image, a matching thought. And after that, well, there was no stopping me.

SHERIDAN: You're a poet!

PAMELA: *(Looking away)* Yes, . . . I guess I am.

SHERIDAN: How long?

PAMELA: Two years.

SHERIDAN: Why didn't you tell me?

PAMELA: When? You were never here. And when you were, you were always a million miles away, probably thinking about your precious play. *(As she picks the papers up and gently puts them back in her basket)* And my poems, they kept me company, gave me solace. My poetry was something I didn't have to share with anyone.

SHERIDAN: Not even me?

PAMELA: *(An edge)* Especially not you.

SHERIDAN: I see. *(They look at each other for a moment. Then, with disdain)* So—what are they about, your poems?

PAMELA: *(Tenderly)* Love, loss, unrequited love. *(Then, with disdain)* And your play?

SHERIDAN: Love. Lost love. It's the story of a married couple who can barely stand to be with each other in the same room anymore. Something had happened two years earlier; an incident, a betrayal.

PAMELA: Betrayal?

SHERIDAN: That they both knew about but never acknowledged. A dark secret that tore them apart. *(Then, smiling)* It's a two-character comedy.

PAMELA: A comedy, you're kidding?

SHERIDAN: No, it's an absurd comedy. The humor comes out of the pain. The play is filled with hidden meanings; the pain is in the subtext.

PAMELA: I see.

SHERIDAN: So are all your poems sad?

PAMELA: Tragic, each and every one.

SHERIDAN: What are they about?

PAMELA: Regrets.

SHERIDAN: Regrets?

PAMELA: And the loneliness that comes from lies. And about apologies, thought about, but never actually made.

SHERIDAN: How sad.

PAMELA: How does your play end?

SHERIDAN: You'll have to read it to find out.

PAMELA: You'd let me? I'd love to. When?

SHERIDAN: *(Backing off)* I don't know, we'll see, someday.

PAMELA: And maybe someday I'll let you read some of my poems.

SHERIDAN: You would? I'd like that.

PAMELA: Would you?

SHERIDAN: Very much.

PAMELA: And who knows, maybe, maybe someday we could even "collaborate" on something.

SHERIDAN: Collaborate?

PAMELA: Sure, why not?

SHERIDAN: Maybe . . . someday. *(THEY look at each other for a moment. Then . . .)* But for now I prefer working alone.

PAMELA: *(Sitting down in the chair)* So do I. *(She starts knitting again. HE starts to leave)* Where are you going?

SHERIDAN: *(HE stops)* To the bathroom.

PAMELA: Oh, I see. Well don't let me stop you.—Your faucet is waiting!

HE looks at her, then leaves. SHE watches him go. After a moment SHE slowly puts the knitting down, sadly looks up, takes out some paper and a pen. Just as she begins to write, SHERIDAN appears in the doorway. She puts the pen and paper down by her side.

PAMELA: What, what is it?

SHERIDAN: *(Softly)* I realized—I don't have to go to the bathroom.

PAMELA: *(With hope)* No?

SHERIDAN: No.

SHE looks down at the pen and paper next to her for a moment, then looks back up at SHERIDAN. SHERIDAN sits down. They look at each other for a moment. Then, slowly, we notice just a hint of a smile appear on their faces, as the lights fade.

END OF PLAY

Creating *The Pain in the Poetry*

by Glenn Alterman

For me, it all started with the one line "I wrote a play." I have no idea where that opening line originated, but it somehow became like a bullet shot from a gun. I put it down on paper. I looked at it. And then a response line came to me: "Hm, what?" At that point, I had an image in my mind, a woman sitting in a chair, sewing. In that image she didn't seemed too concerned about what the first speaker had said. She was too preoccupied with sewing. That made me go back to the first line and add the stage directions "Meekly, softly." So now I saw this gentle man speaking to his perhaps more dominant wife. I could see him as small in stature and a bit oppressed by his wife. He repeats the line, but this time more boldly: "I said, I wrote a play." There was something about the way he responds that opened up the dynamic of these two characters for me. I always feel that artists are bold when they create something from nothing. In this moment of the play, she is like an authoritative mother figure. There were echoes of George and Martha (from *Who's Afraid of Virginia Woolf*) floating through my mind. I instinctively knew I didn't want to quite go in that direction. But I knew I wanted there to be contention between these two characters, some underlying anger or ambivalence toward each other. It was the first clue I had to their relationship. The way that I could express her passive-aggressive behavior toward him was to be dismissive with her line "That's nice dear, did you feed the dog?" Angered by her dismissive tone, Sheridan stands up for himself (and his art) as he gets more riled up by her next disinterested comments. And that dynamic continues in tandem with the revelations about his secret life writing a play. I realized that this was not going to be a realistic play, so I let myself imagine how Sheridan has been secretly writing his play for two years. I connected with my own feelings when I get possessed writing a play and let the absurdities go as far as they could. Her surprise, even shock, added the drama and comedy in the scene. I realized I had to be deadly serious with all this to make it funny; life-and-death funny. I avoided easy jokes and references about playwriting as much as I could, and went for his passion and truth, moment by moment.

As the play progressed it felt one-sided; all the energy was about him, his secretive playwriting and her shock and acceptance of what he'd been doing. His writing of the play and admission of it was like that of a husband finally revealing that he's been having an affair; but in this case the affair was writing of the play. All of the references, sexual and otherwise, applied to his clandestine secret life as a playwright.

It is his admission that he's thinking of writing another play (i.e., another affair) that prompts her to get up and threaten to leave him. At this point I had no idea what would happen. But as she stood up and the papers from her basket fell the idea came that perhaps she too had a secret life. At first I believe I thought she might also reveal that she was a playwright. But I felt I had mined all the humor I could with his revelations about playwriting. I'm not sure where the idea of her being a poet came into play. I don't know that much about poetry writing. But I went with it, and through her dialogue I realized I knew more about poetry than I thought I did. And now she had to match his references about playwriting to hers about poetry. The obvious reference in the real world is the wife admitting that she too has been having an affair, after her husband has revealed that he had been unfaithful. I allowed the two of them to equate their art with the same passion based on the same pain and revealed past real life indiscretions—the idea being that in both their cases their art came out of their pain and loneliness. The idea that art comes from pain is one many people believe to be truthful, and I allowed that cliché to be the center of these two characters' universe.

After all the cards were on the table I needed to end my play. I was getting close to my ten-page limit. I had already worked through the first draft and continued with rewrites, so I had several endings, as I usually do. For a while I had him leave and that was it. I wanted ambiguity as to whether their life and marriage could ever come together. Then, perhaps in a better frame of mind, I had him return. I like the tension of that moment, not knowing why he's returned—then her asking why he came back. And his simplistic answer, "I realized I didn't have to go to the bathroom." The line has several meanings. It is in the following stage direction, "we notice just a hint of a smile appear on their faces, as the lights fade," that I tip my hand a bit more with just the possibility of hope and reconciliation. I found that a more satisfying ending.

Chapter 14

Where to Submit Your Ten-Minute Play

There are literally hundreds of theaters that are looking for ten-minute plays for festivals. Many are very well-known theater companies, and others are community theaters, amateur theater companies, local church groups, etc. Then, too, there are hundreds of ten-minute playwriting competitions, many offering substantial prizes. It seems each year more and more theaters and contests are appearing on playwriting Web sites. If you start researching you'll find a plethora of possibilities for that new ten-minute play you worked so hard on. But you must be proactive and submit your little gem.

Be systematic and keep accurate records of where and when you submitted your play. You might keep a folder, as I do, entitled "Ten-Minute Play Submissions." In that folder you should include for each submission:

- The name, address, and/or Web site of the theater company
- The name of the specific person you contacted, if any
- The name of the play(s) you submitted
- If it was a contest, the name of the competition, and the prize offered
- When the company stated their results would be decided
- A record of any prizes or honors you won with your submission (including finalist standing)

What follows is just a sampling of theater companies and contests that accept ten-minute plays. I could list many more, but I have space limitations in this book. The list is made up of places I've had personal dealings with, as well as those I've heard about through friends who recommend them.

Always check to make sure any listing's information is accurate, as there may be changes from year to year.

Some of these play submission requirements come directly from the theaters' Web sites; others in response to my inquiries. You'll notice that some of the submission guidelines are detailed, while others basically just say, send your play along.

Ten-Minute Play Festivals

Boston Playwright's Theater
Attn: Boston Theater Marathon
949 Commonwealth Avenue
Boston, MA 02215
617-353-5443

Submission Guidelines:

- To submit your ten-minute play for this competition, you must be a permanent resident of New England.
- All scripts must play under ten minutes.
- Please use a 10-point font or larger.
- No more than two submissions per author.
- Minimal sets and props suggested.
- There are no restrictions on subject matter.
- Scripts must be typewritten in accepted playwriting format (the theater refers authors to the Samuel French Formatting Guide, available at www.samuelfrench.com/submissions, the essentials of which are covered in Chapter 5 of this book).
- You must submit three copies of each script. Please put the title on the first page of each copy, but no author name.
- Please only staple the top left on each copy. All other covers, ring bindings, etc. will be removed.
- Submit a single separate information page for each play that you enter. On the separate page include the title of the play, the playwright's name, the address (including e-mail address), and your phone numbers.
- Please do not staple the information page to your scripts.
- Scripts will not be returned.
- Send your scripts and information to the above address.

Celebration Theatre
Mailing address:
7895 Santa Monica Boulevard, #109-1
Los Angeles, CA 90046

Physical address:
7051 Santa Monica Boulevard
Los Angeles, CA 90038
323-957-1884
info@celebrationtheatre.com
www.celebrationtheatre.com

Celebration Theatre looks for innovative, provocative, relevant work that examines the gay, lesbian, bisexual, transgender, and queer experience. Their mission statement is to endeavor to challenge society's perception of the GLBT community and to give a vibrant voice to its evolving identity.

Submission Guidelines:

- Download and complete the submission packet at www.celebration-theatre.com/literary.html.
- Submit the packet to the mailing address above, including
  ○ A bound copy of the script
  ○ A character breakdown
  ○ A cover letter
  ○ A self-addressed stamped envelope, if you desire the return of your submission packet.

Theatre Oxford Ten-Minute Play Contest
PO Box 1394
Oxford, MS 38655

Submission Guidelines:

- Only original plays, never before produced, are eligible.
- The play, exclusive of title and cast pages, may be no more than ten pages.
- The play should have two to four characters and minimal props and costumes.

- Assemble script as follows:
  - Two copies of the play.
  - Optional cover letter.
  - A title page with the play's title, author's name, address, phone number, and e-mail address. This is the only place that the author's name should appear.
  - The second page should contain a cast of characters and time and place information.
  - The third page will be the first page of the script. The other pages of the play follow.
  - Every page should include the name of the play and page number.
- The play, exclusive of title and cast pages, may be no more than ten pages.
- Staple or paper-clip the play. Do not use binders or folders of any kind.
- Authors may submit multiple plays, but each play submitted must be accompanied by the submission of an entry fee.
- There is an entry fee of $10. Make check out to Theatre Oxford. The fee must accompany each entry.
- Mail entries to the address above. Plays cannot be returned. Enclose a SASP if you want assurance that your play was received.
- Only the five finalists will be notified of judging results. All plays are judged blind.
- Five finalists will be chosen. The Grand Prize Winner will receive the L. W. Thomas Award of $1,000 and a production of the winning script.
- All authors agree to permit Theatre Oxford to produce their contest entry play if the theater should wish to do so. Authors retain copyright and full ownership of their plays.

Chicago Dramatists
1105 West Chicago Avenue
Chicago, IL 60622
312-633-0630
www.chicagodramatists.org

Submission Guidelines:

- Playwrights may submit no more than one piece to each workshop.
- Submissions must be ten pages or less.

- Standard 12-point font size, pages numbered.
- Plays should not contain more than six characters.
- No musicals, binding, staples, faxes, or e-mailed submissions are accepted, and submissions will not be returned.
- A submitting playwright must include his or her day and evening phone numbers and a character list with ages.
- Submission rules and deadlines are announced in the theater's quarterly flyers and on its Web site.

Actors Theatre of Louisville
National Ten-Minute Play Contest
316 West Main Street
Louisville, KY 40202-4218
502-584-1265
actorstheatre.org

Certainly one of the most famous ten-minute play contests is held at the Actors Theatre of Louisville. Their New Play Program encompasses the Humana Festival of New American Plays, the National Ten-Minute Play Contest, and ongoing contact with more than 200 playwrights. Approximately 2,000 scripts are received annually for consideration in the New Play Program. Nearly 75,000 scripts have been submitted since 1976.

Beginning in 2011, they redirected the focus of the contest toward the primary production opportunity for ten-minute plays at Actors Theatre: the Apprentice/Intern Tens. An annual event that takes place in January, the A/I Tens consist of a bill of eight to ten world premiere ten-minute plays, fully produced in Actors' Victor Jory Theatre and performed by their Apprentice Company of young actors.

As a result of this refocusing and their individual programming needs, Actors Theatre of Louisville and City Theatre of Miami will no longer cosponsor the National Ten-Minute Play Contest, though each theater will separately continue its commitment to finding and producing excellent ten-minute plays, and getting to know the work of writers around the country. Playwrights who wish to submit a ten-minute play to be considered for City Theatre's Summer Shorts Festival should visit www.citytheatre.com for more information.

Submission Guidelines:

- Characters in submitted plays should be 18 to 28 years of age.
- Submissions will be limited to the first 500 scripts received each year: scripts will only be accepted during a focused submission window between September 1 and November 1.
- Contestants whose plays are received within this time frame but after the 500-script mark will be notified.
- Entries will be acknowledged by postcard in December. Playwrights will be notified of their finalist or non-finalist status the following summer.
- Each playwright may submit only one script.
- Electronic submissions are not accepted.
- No scripts will be returned.
- Each script must be no more than ten pages long (not including the title page and character list).
- Previously submitted plays, plays that have received an Equity production, musicals, children's shows, and any unsolicited longer one-act or full-length plays are not accepted and will not be returned or acknowledged. Plays that have received Equity waiver showcase productions are eligible.
- Each manuscript must be typed and individually bound or stapled. The title page must include the playwright's name, address, phone number and e-mail address.
- All ten-minute plays will be considered for the Heideman Award ($1000) and production in the Apprentice/Intern Tens, an annual event in the winter.
- Playwrights must be citizens or permanent residents of the USA.

Queer Shorts c/o StageQ
113 E. Mifflin Street
Madison, WI 53703
www.stageq.com

Plays should be no longer than 15 minutes. Please send no more than three scripts, and do not resubmit scripts that you have sent in the past. You can e-mail your script and précis to QueerShorts@stageq.com. They have a strong preference for receiving scripts electronically, but if that's not possible, you may send them via snail mail to the address above.

Submission Guidelines:

Please include a one-page précis, including:

- One-paragraph description of the plot.
- Casting requirements (number of actors, gender, ages, special requirements, if any).
- Set requirements (since this is a playfest with 10–12 plays in one evening; simple is better!).
- Running time (no more than 15 minutes!).
- Special technical requirements, if any.
- Who is the intended audience?
- Is there lesbian, gay or other queer content?
- Is there nudity? Adult language?
- If a musical, is there a written score?
- If a musical, what are the instrumental requirements? Vocal requirements?

The festival acknowledges all scripts received and generally notifies winners by early April. Plays are performed at the Bartell Theatre in Madison, Wisconsin.

Drama Ministry
PO Box 40387
Nashville, TN 37204
www.dramaministry.com

Drama Ministry is looking for scripts that can be used in worship services to focus the attention of worshipers on specific themes or life issues that the pastor can then address in the sermon or message that follows.

Submission Guidelines:

- Please be sure to have your script formatted according to our script style sheet (see Web site).
- Sketches should be from four to seven minutes long and use one to six characters.
- Include a statement of purpose, time requirements, list of characters, prop list, and any unusual sound or light requirements.
- Scripts should be sensitive to the un-churched. Avoid Christian-club jargon and insider church terminology.

- Must have broad appeal to both evangelical and mainline audiences.
- Most of our scripts are not obviously religious in nature. Rather, they pose human situations that can be addressed from the pulpit following the sketch.
- No elaborate staging or costumes.
- Problems should be identified without sarcasm or overly critical tones (hope-based vs. critique-based). We do not want scripts that scold the audience or try to shame the viewers. Scripts that ridicule the hypocrisy of Christians are not for us.
- Avoid didactic lines. Specifically, avoid making "less spiritual" characters mere foils who present questions and/or problems for "more spiritual" characters to resolve as "teachers. "
- We prefer everyday situations to extreme situations.
- Avoid predictable endings: we prefer a conclusion that is unexpected but still a reasonable extension of the theme of the sketch.
- Put your name and address on your script.
- Please note that your submission will not be returned.

Turtle Shell Productions: 8-Minute Madness Playwright Festival
300 W. 43rd Street #403
New York, NY 10036
www.turtleshellproductions.com

Turtle Shell Productions accepts eight- to ten-minute plays for their festival. The selected plays, which will be presented in two groups of 11, will be directed by carefully selected directors, performed by New York actors, and mounted by a team of experienced set, lighting, sound, and costume designers.

The 11 plays in Group A will be performed by adult actors (though a child actor may be included, if needed). The 11 plays in Group B will be performed by young actors (ages 9–17) as part of a separate presentation on an alternate night. At the end of the run, the recipients of the Best Playwright and Best Performance awards will receive the 8-Minute Madness Playwright Festival Trophies at the Artist Celebration Awards Ceremonies.

Submission Guidelines:

- The front cover should include the play's title and the playwright's name, address, phone number, and email address.

- Include a page with the character breakdown.
- Script pages should be numbered and the text presented in an acceptable format.
- If you would like to be notified that your script has been received, include a self-addressed stamped postcard.
- Plays must be ten minutes or less in duration. Be prepared to shorten them if necessary.
- There is no fee for submitting your play(s).
- Plays that have been produced under an "Equity Code" are acceptable but must be identified on the application with the dates of production. We are also accept plays that have been produced before or have had a reading.
- Each playwright may submit up to two plays. (Please note on the application which is your first submission and which is your second.)
- Please include your application with play submission.
- No electronic submissions.
- If you have any questions, please contact the Festival Selection Committee at 8minute@turtleshellproductions.com.

Heartland Theater Company Ten-Minute Play Festival
PO Box 1833
Bloomington, IL 61702-1833
309-452-8709
www.heartlandtheatre.org

Heartland Theatre Company is seeking original plays to be considered for production as part of their annual ten-minute play festival. Please see their website for the yearly theme.

Submission Guidelines:

- Submit entries electronically in Microsoft Word, formatted following their style sheet (see website).
- Plays must be new. Please do not send anything that has previously been produced.
- Please use no more than four characters and no fewer than two.
- Please make sure that your characters can be played by actors between the ages of 18 and 70.

- Your play should consist mainly of dialogue. Ten-minute monologues will not be accepted.
- No children's plays, musicals, or plays previously staged by Heartland Theatre will be considered.
- Do not put your name on the play itself, as all submissions are judged blind.
- Make sure the title of the play appears on every page of the play.
- Only one entry per playwright.
- Your play must be written in English.
- All entrants must complete and submit the Heartland Theatre Ten-Minute Play Festival Entry Form in order to submit a play.

NYCPlaywrights Short Plays
nycp.blogspot.com

The theme for the plays changes yearly, so contact them directly.

Submission Guidelines:

- Send only one ten-minute play per author to info@nycplaywrights .org.
- Attach your script to your submission e-mail in Microsoft Word or as a pdf.
- The script can be no longer than ten pages (not including title page, setting info page, etc.).
- The script should be in standard playscript format. If you are not sure what that is, see this page on the NYCPlaywrights Web site: nycp.blogspot.com/p/playscript-formatting-template.html.
- Plays that are not in standard format, or that have more than ten pages (not counting title page, etc.), will be rejected immediately.
- Make sure you have your name and your e-mail address on the title page of the script.
- Plays can be from anybody, anywhere in the world, but must be primarily in English (a few non-English phrases are acceptable, but the phrases must include English translations in production notes or stage directions.)
- There is no fee for submission and no payment given for the plays selected. Do not send a submission if you are expecting monetary compensation.

- The NYCPlaywrights selection decision is final and NYCPlaywrights reserves the right to select no plays from those submitted.
- The play must have been written by the person making the submission.
- The play can have had a previous production but cannot have been published.
- All rights will remain with the playwright.
- The selected play will be videotaped as a reading during an NYCPlaywrights meeting and posted shortly after, during the month of November.
- The video recording of the play reading will be posted to the NYCPlaywrights YouTube account and from there embedded into the NYCPlaywrights blog. The embedded section may be an excerpt of the play reading rather than the entire reading. The playwright will be asked to review the video recording and approve it before it is made public.
- The play must reflect the month's theme in some meaningful way.
- The readings that are recorded are actual script-in-hand readings, not productions. To get an idea of what to expect for the final product, see the page on the NYCPlaywrights Web site with samples of past readings of Plays of the Month: nycp.blogspot.com/p/play-of-month.html.

Newburgh Free Academy Drama Department
201 Fullerton Avenue
Newburgh, NY 12550

The Newburgh Free Academy is an at-risk high school located in Hudson Valley, New York. The students will be in charge of reading, acting, designing, directing, and producing chosen work.

Submission Guidelines:

- Plays must be ten minutes or less.
- Playwrights may submit up to two plays only.
- Plays must be unpublished.
- Plays that have had productions, workshops, or readings are allowed.
- No electronic submissions.
- Send to the attention of Terry Sandler at the address above.

- There is no submission fee, although there is a suggested donation of $1.00 per play. Make checks out to Newburgh Enlarged City Schools. The money will be used for the drama club account to buy props and other supplies for the festival.

Stone Soup Theatre
c/o Double (XX) Fest
4035 Stone Way N.
Seattle, WA 98103
203-633-1883
www.stonesouptheatre.org

Stone Soup Theatre is seeking one-act plays 3–25 minutes in length, original and unpublished (though they may have been previously produced), with minimal set, costumes, and characters, and particularly ten-minute shorts written by women. If you are interested in and capable of putting together the production as well (finding directors, actors, and/or costume and props resources), please include this information in your cover letter.

Submission Guidelines:
- One submission per playwright only.
- E-mail submissions preferred: playfestival@stonesouptheatre.org.
- If you must submit by snail mail, please use the address above.
- Include a separate cover containing contact information, mailing address, phone number, and a brief description of authorial intent.
- The cover page should include the play title, author's name, character list/description, gender breakdown, genre, and a brief description of the play.
- All mentions of author's name /contact must be removed from the body of the play.
- Submissions, both electronic and snail mail, must include (incomplete or incorrect submissions will be disqualified).
- There is no fee, but donations are welcome.

Salve Regina Theatre Arts Program
Salve Regina University
100 Ochre Point Avenue
Newport, RI 02840-4192
401-847-6650

Salve Regina University Theatre Arts program seeks submissions of ten-minute plays and full-length play scripts for their weeklong festival. The play committee will choose 8–12 plays for performance during the festival with the audience favorite receiving a cash prize. One play will be chosen for a workshop production in the Casino Theatre. A short rehearsal process will take place prior to the festival and the winning playwright will be encouraged to attend and make edits.

Submission Guidelines:

- Mail a copy of your script to the Theatre Arts program at Salve Regina University.
- There is no submission fee.
- Playwrights should submit work that has not been previously produced; however, plays that have received readings will be accepted.
- The ten-minute play category is open to all playwrights and all genres of scripts.
- You can submit your ten-minute plays electronically to https://salvetheatreplayfestival.submittable.com/submit.

Trinity Church Playwrights Competition
74 Trinity Place, 23rd Floor
New York, NY 10006
212-602-0800
www.trinitywallstreet.org

Trinity Church Arts Committee is seeking unproduced and unpublished one-act plays of no longer than 30 pages. The first-prize winner will receive $500 and earn a reading of his or her play. The second-place winner will receive $200 and the third-place winner will receive $100.

Submission Guidelines:

- There is no entry fee.
- The play must be submitted via e-mail in Microsoft Word format to ArtsCommittee@trinitywallstreet.org.
- Only one submission per playwright.

The Fine Arts Association
38660 Mentor Avenue
Willoughby, OH 44094
440-951-7500

The Fine Arts Association is looking for original, never-published ten-minute plays. Those chosen will be fully produced as part of their Annual One Act Festival.

Submission Guidelines:

- Submissions must be original, unpublished, and unproduced ten-minute plays at time of submission.
- Plays that have had staged readings will be accepted.
- Plays that have received full productions, either professional or amateur, previous to submission will not be accepted.
- Legal clearance of materials not in the public domain is the full responsibility of the playwright.
- There is no limit to the number of plays submitted by each playwright.
- Maximum length: ten pages, not including title pages.
- Scripts may be comedy or drama. Musicals are not eligible.
- Set and technical requirements must be minimal: only standard furniture and minimal props will be available for the production.
- Plays must be typed/word-processed with pages numbered and include a cover page with the following contact information: your name, address, phone number, e-mail address, and a brief biography.

Mail submissions to the address above. Submissions must be securely bound with a cover page with full contact information (see above). If you mail your script and would like it returned, include an SASE with your submission.

Submissions may be e-mailed to ahedger@fineartsassociation.org and should include a separate page with full contact information. Preferred document format: Microsoft Word (.doc or .docx) or pdf files.

Towne Street Theatre Annual Ten-Minute Play Festival
Towne Street Theatre
4101 Budlong Avenue #4
Los Angeles, CA 90037
213-712-6944
www.townestreet.org

Towne Street Theatre is LA's premiere African American theater company. The festival will take place during Black History Month, at the Stella Adler

Theatre in Hollywood. Each year there is a different theme, so check their website for information.

Submission Guidelines:

- All genres are welcome: comedy, drama, satire, etc.
- Plays can be historical, contemporary, or futuristic, with color-blind and/or multiracial casts.
- Playwrights of all ethnicities and ages are encouraged to submit their work.
- There is no processing fee, but please do not submit more than one play.
- Please make sure your play is only ten minutes in length.

Longwood Ten-Minute Play Festival
English Department
Longwood University
201 High Street
Farmville, VA 23909
434-395-2000

Longwood University is open to any theme, style, and approach. Playwrights are invited to submit a maximum of one script. All winners, as well as one honorable mention, will receive publication with One Act Play Depot. One Act Play Depot will hold non-exclusive rights to the work (meaning playwrights are free to publish their work elsewhere at any time). Please note that anyone affiliated with Longwood University—students, former students, employees and their families—is ineligible for this competition.

Submission Guidelines:

- Scripts should run no longer than ten minutes.
- Stapled copies are fine.
- Set and technical requirements should be minimal.
- Each script must include the author's contact information on its cover page.
- There is no fee to enter.
- Please send plays (hard copies only) to the address above.

Salem Theater Company Moments of Play Ten-Minute Play Festival
90 Lafayette Street
PO Box 306
Salem, MA 01970
978-790-8546
www.salemtheatre.com

Salem Theater Company is looking for pieces that are culturally diverse, original, fun, and relevant. Playwrights whose plays are chosen for production will receive a $10 royalty for each of the five performances given ($50 total).

Submission Guidelines:

- Playwrights may submit up to two plays.
- Plays must be no more than ten minutes in length and have no more than four characters.
- All plays must be submitted electronically in pdf format to mop@salemtheatre.com.
- Plays received via post office will be unable to be considered and will not be returned.

Universal Theatre
PO Box 1818
Provincetown, MA 02657
www.universaltheatre.com

Universal Theatre is seeking ten-minute plays (no more than ten pages), preferably with no more than three characters. Also seeking monologues (no more than four pages).

Submission Guidelines:

- No more than two submissions per playwright.
- Please do not resubmit plays already submitted.
- Please no SASE.
- No binders, covers, boxes, bells & bows, etc. Simply use a staple or paper clip to contain scripts.
- No press or bios. The work will speak for itself.

- Submit to the address above.

Figgy Pudding Play Festival
Unity Stage Company
917-548-1086
unitystagecompany@gmail.com

Unity Stage Company in Queens, New York, seeks short plays (5 to 25 minutes in length) on the theme of Christmas for their Figgy Pudding Play Festival.

Submission Guidelines:

- Please submit a short play with the following qualities:
  - Unsentimental dialogue
  - Unique, well-drawn characters
  - Surprising plot twist(s)
  - Funny/edgy
  - New insights into the significance of this holiday and its "trimmings"
  - Must be unpublished but may have had a prior production
- There is no limit on the number of plays submitted per playwright.
- Please e-mail your script to us at unitystagecompany@gmail.com.

InspiraTO Playwriting Contest
www.inspiratofestival.ca

Each year the InspiraTO Festival accepts ten-minute play submissions based on a theme. If selected, your play will be performed in Toronto, Canada. Between 10 and 18 ten-minute plays will be selected and performed. 1st Prize: $500 CDN.

Should your play be selected for inclusion in the festival, you are giving the non-exclusive right to Theatre InspiraTO to produce and perform the play in the Seventh Annual InspiraTO Festival. The InspiraTO Festival will find the cast and crew and market your play.

Submission Guidelines:

- We accept previously produced plays.
- Any style is acceptable except musicals.
- Submissions are open to everyone without age and geographic restriction.
- Play must not be shorter than eight minutes and not longer than ten minutes.
- There is no submission fee.
- You may only enter ONE play (so make it count).
- To submit your play, view this year's themes and fill out the submission form at http://www.inspiratofestival.ca/write-a-play.php.
- Attach your script in a Word document or in a pdf file. The Word document must be compatible with Window XP. (Note: Vista and Mac formats are not compatible.)
- The cover page should have the title of the play, the playwright's name, and the list of characters.
- The pages should be numbered.

Publishers of Ten-Minute Plays

Playscripts, Inc.
450 Seventh Avenue, Suite 809
New York, NY 10123
866-639-7529
www.playscripts.com/submit

Electronic submissions are strongly preferred. While Playscripts does publish and license musicals, the limitations of time and staff prevent them from accepting unsolicited musical submissions. They do not accept screenplays.

Smith & Kraus Publishers, Inc.
PO Box 127
Lyme, NH 03768
207-523-2585
www.smithkraus.com

They request that you send a query letter and synopsis of your play. They'll get back to you in a few weeks.

Heuer Publishing LLC
PO Box 248
Cedar Rapids, IA 52406
www.hitplays.com

Before you submit your work to Heuer, familiarize yourself with their market and follow the guidelines listed on their Web site. Due to the large volume of submissions that they receive daily, please limit your submissions to three at any given time.

Brooklyn Publishers LLC
Submissions:
Brooklyn Publishers
Attn: Editor
5213 New Orleans Drive
Odessa, TX 79762

Physical address:
211 First Avenue SE, Suite 200
Cedar Rapids, IA 52401
Toll Free: 1-888-473-8521
www.brookpub.com

Brooklyn publishes plays and theater books for teens and youth, special-
izing in scripts that are clean yet have a cutting-edge quality. The range of
genres they publish is broad and includes comedy, drama, mystery, fantasy,
farce, and melodrama.

Submission Guidelines:

- Authors are encouraged to send submissions via the publisher's Web
  site, by clicking on **Submit a Play** in the Author's Corner on the left
  border.
- You may also submit a play by e-mail with attachment at editor@
  brookpub.com or by snail-mail with a complete manuscript to the
  Texas address above.
- When you submit a play, please include the following:
  - Short synopsis of the work
  - The play's genre, duration, and cast size
  - Character list
  - Production history (if any; not required)
  - Short bio of the playwright
  - Contact information, including e-mail address, phone number,
    and mailing address
- Microsoft Word and Adobe Acrobat are the preferred text process-
  ing programs; however, if you use another program please use Rich
  Text Format (rtf).

Chapter 15

Observations about the Ten-Minute Play

Anastasia Traina, Playwright

One secret I'd like to share is, if you can write a one minute play or a ten-minute play you can write a full-length play. The structure is exactly the same. There is always a beginning, a middle, and, of course, your grand finale. Sounds simple, right? It is, if you follow a few rules, or at least know them so that you may toss them to the wind if need be (for the sake of your artistic expression).

Here are some rules that I find quite handy: first, I ask myself *the* question, "Why is this night different than any other night?" Then I jump right into my story. I like to keep my audience guessing, but I never want them to feel lost. Remember: we are all drawn in by the unknown, but too many unknowns lead to a distracted audience.

Then there is the little thing I like to call action, action, and then more action, meaning, keep it tight and moving. There is absolutely no time for long ramblings or dawdles that would diminish your already flowered words! Meaning, every word counts, builds, and develops your story! Also, a very good thing to remember is that all characters have *dreams, wants, and needs*. These things are what make your character one-of-a-kind and most importantly memorable. His or her hopes and ambitions will hopefully drive them to the climax of your play.

And finally, for me, the most important part of the play is . . . will my character win or lose? Will all the struggles have been worth the journey—a journey that will inevitably bring the characters back to where they started but with an awareness that changes them forever?

Scott C. Sickles, Artistic Director, WorkShop Theater Company, New York City

Ten-minute plays are a special breed of one-act. The restriction of telling a story in 600 seconds provides the author with the kind of pressure and motivations he or she should instill in the story and characters.

Ten-minute plays also offer playwrights a certain freedom to explore and experiment with form, structure, content. They're about capturing a moment in time—or out of time in some cases—allowing the writer to try a new genre, find a new voice from within, and build a new universe, without having to sustain these new laws of physics over two acts.

Likewise, a playwright can opt to tell a traditional story—beginning, middle, end—but without the burden of creating a status quo interrupted by an inciting incident causing the protagonist to go on a journey where the action rises into a crisis that leads to a decision resulting in a climactic confrontation settling into a denouement, but rather just hitting the crisis and the climax with maybe shavings of rising action and a denouement on the fringes. One doesn't have time for a lot of exposition in ten minutes. You hit the ground running and you go.

When I'm looking at short plays at the WorkShop Theater Company and at ten-minute plays specifically, I still look for strong characters in a strong story. Those characters may be familiar or original. The story may be traditional or bizarre. (I kind of enjoy familiar characters in a bizarre story or inspired characters in a traditional setting.) But whatever the story is, it must be engaging, moving in some way (laughter, tears, in between), active (not a couple of people talking about offstage stuff unless they have a really good reason), focused on a singular event (I myself have tried to write the ten-minute epic tale of a town, three families, and how their lives have all changed over generations—I exaggerate, but only a little), and most importantly not preachy. I feel this way about plays of any length, but in ten-minute play, platitudes become fortune cookies. If the characters are talking about an issue, make it specific, give them a reason, get to the heart of the characters and their passions and leave the message unsaid until someone *has* to say it. Give your actors something to do besides talk and pose. Make them love, fight, die, rejoice, befuddle, and engage like they have ten minutes to live, because they do!

But ultimately, the piece must entertain. An important message in a boring package is boring and no one hears the message. If you're going to be avant-garde, at least do it in a way that makes sense—give us a window so we can see into the beautiful, strange world you created. We are writing to amuse others, not just ourselves. Write a play that the audience wishes went on for another two hours. A good ten-minute play will leave us satisfied and wanting more. Though that's probably true for most plays, it's especially true here.

Dirk Knef, Literary Advisor, After Folsom Festival (Berlin, Germany) and others

I read hundreds of ten-minute plays every year from playwrights all over the world for different ten-minute play festivals in Germany, Barcelona, and Prague. The plays vary from sketch-like, underdeveloped plays to overly detailed, too-many-story-lined plays.

I want something that will grab me by the end of the first page (at the least) and take me on a whirlwind adventure. I suppose what I'm saying is that I want to be engaged as early as possible with your play. I want to care about your characters (not too many!) and be invested in the story you're telling. And lastly, I don't want to feel "dumped" at the end of your ten-minute play. It seems so many plays I read just "end." Either that or I am hit with what the playwright (I suppose) feels is a last-minute shocker or "twist." I'm all for the O. Henry surprise in a ten-minute play, but make sure all the events in your play lead to it.

Suzanne Bradbeer, Playwright

I love the immediacy of the short play. It's a great training ground for getting your conflict front and center quickly. You can't be coy about what your play is about when you've only got ten pages to tell your story. And no chatting, no matter how charming you think that chatting is! This is true with longer plays too, but it becomes particularly clear in a ten-minute play that your characters should speak because they dearly want something from someone. "Getting to know you" dialogue quickly loses our interest, as does "Remember when . . . "

I've also found that writing the ten-minute play is a fun way to get to work with some of my favorite actors—many of my short plays have been written and produced for specific people.

Eduardo Arbo, Playwright, Barcelona

How can a playwright not love writing ten-minute plays? They create a whole universe in only ten minutes. And while a person might struggle for months or years on a full-length play, the ten-minute play doesn't take forever to complete. That being said, you must give it as much of your creative energy and imagination as you would to a full length play. It's still has the same rules of playwriting.

As with many of my plays, I allow my dreams to participate in my creation. Dreams are a passageway to your subconscious. I find that sometimes a mini-dream moment, when either I'm just falling asleep or just about to wake up, gives me a gem for a ten-minute play. It may be an image in the dream or a short scene in the dream that inspires some thought for the play. I keep a journal; perhaps you should try that. You'll find there's never a shortage of plot ideas.

The characters for ten-minute plays must be as rich and fully developed as those in your full-length plays. I do recommend fewer characters for the ten-minute play and if possible, only one set.

Elaine Romero, Playwright

I love ten-minute plays. Many playwrights say they feel a greater freedom in writing the ten-minute play over other lengths. Writing daring ten-minute plays became a bridge for me to take greater risks in my full-length work. So why did I initially experience a greater risk with the ten-minute play? The reason was twofold. I think it had to do, in part, with the audience's willingness to accept whatever world the playwright presents in the short form. But it also had to do with my access to my creative ideas, and my willingness to engage in premises that I might have deemed too strange for the longer form.

I remember taking a note in many notebooks before actually writing anything down. The note said, "Don't forget to write the play about the water droplet who falls in love with the lightning bug." Fodder for a full-length play? Probably not. But for a short play, such a premise writes itself.

The audience and the playwright are freer to explore an unexpected world in a ten-minute play. As a result, the ten-minute play can be particularly theatrical. When writing the ten-minute play, consider that you are freer than you would be in any other medium. Yes, even film. Dream of a landscape—a world—that can be self-contained that naturally defies the world that you know. Give that world its own rules. Feel free to break free from realism. Feel free.

If you start writing and you think it's a stupid idea, don't stop. You're onto something new. If you don't recognize it, that's because you're embracing your creativity, your originality. When embarking on new creative territory, your first impulse might be to kill your idea. But ideas are like seeds. You would not look at a seed and tell it, "You're going to grow up to be an ugly tree." Instead, give your ideas a chance to grow to maturity. They deserve that much.

Writing a lot of ten-minute plays can be like creating building blocks for your playwriting. A playwright stands on top of all the plays s/he has written. You may be perfectly satisfied writing ten-minute plays for the rest of your life, or find within them seedlings for longer works. Regardless, the ten-minute play will teach you to dream in ways you've never dreamt before. Dream big.

Chapter 16

And in the End

Hopefully by this point you should have some good ideas and have been inspired to start work on your ten-minute play, if you haven't begun already. One tip: avoid procrastinating and get to it as soon as you can.

Playwrights: Some Key Points to Remember

- Go with your gut, your instincts, for that first draft of your new play. Try to keep out of your head as much as possible.
- Be sure your play has a clear conflict.
- Be certain your characters have clear intentions.
- Avoid unnecessary exposition at all costs.
- Even though it's a ten-minute play, be certain that it has all six elements of drama: plot, character, theme, language, rhythm, and spectacle.
- Be willing to sacrifice a great line(s), a character, a scene, whatever, to keep your story moving efficiently right to the end.
- The ending of your play must be earned, not attached.
- Make sure that your protagonist changes as a result of the conflict he or she encounters in the play.
- Keep stage directions to a minimum.
- Keep your cast to a minimum. Two or three characters are best.
- Keep props and furniture to an absolute minimum.
- Listen to comments and feedback with an open mind. Use what you find useful, but in the end it's your play.
- Make sure your play runs ten minutes.

Some Key Points for Actor/Playwrights

- In general it's best not to be an actor in the first production of your ten-minute play, unless you absolutely feel you must. But be aware there may be limits to your objectivity if rewrites are necessary.
- If possible, don't direct the first production of your ten-minute play. Once again, this will help establish the objectivity you'll need for any rewrites.
- If you have a choice of directors for your play, go with your gut on who seems to understand your play best.
- When you meet with the director, ask him or her to tell you the story of your play and ask how he or she sees it in production.
- After your director has read the play, or has heard you read it aloud, be open to his or her interpretation, especially if it's not quite the same as yours. Try to find a common ground.
- Casting your play is key. Hopefully you and your director will see eye to eye on the best actors for each role. Try not to be too rigid on how you want a role to be cast. Allow for surprises: during auditions, some actors who may not be what you initially had in mind may impress you with their ability to make a role their own. Your director's input can very helpful as you consider the possibility that a role might be played another way.

Selected Bibliography

Here are some suggested books that you may find of value in writing your ten-minute play (as well as writing plays of any length).

Garrison, Gary. *Perfect Ten: Writing and Producing the Ten-Minute Play.* Portsmouth, NH: Heinemann, 2001.

———. *A More Perfect Ten.* Boston: Focus, 2008.

Harbison, Lawrence, ed. *2009: The Best Ten-Minute Plays for Two or More Actors.* Portland, ME: Smith & Kraus, 2009.

Lajos, Egri. *The Art of Dramatic Writing.* New York: Simon & Schuster, 1960.

Rico, Gabriele. *Writing the Natural Way.* New York: Tarcher/Penguin, 1983, 2002. www.gabrielerico.com.

Sweet, Jeffrey. *The Dramatist's Toolkit: The Craft of the Working Playwright.* Portsmouth, NH: Heinemann, 1993.

About the Author

Glenn Alterman is a multi-award-winning playwright, the author of twenty-five theater-related books (including eight books of original monologues), a screenwriter, an actor, and a highly respected monologue/audition acting coach.

His books include *An Actor's Guide—Making It in New York* (and a completely revised second edition), *The Perfect Audition Monologue, Two Minutes and Under (Original Monologues for Actors, Volumes 1, 2, and 3), Street Talk (Original Character Monologues for Actors), Uptown (More Original Monologues for Actors), Glenn Alterman's Secrets to Successful Cold Readings, Sixty Seconds to Shine—101 One-Minute Monologues, Creating Your Own Monologue, Promoting Your Acting Career, The Job Book: One Hundred Acting Jobs for Actors, The Job Book 2: One Hundred Day Jobs for Actors, What to Give Your Agent for Christmas,* and *Two-Minute Monologues. Two Minutes and Under, Street Talk,* and *Uptown,* all number one best-selling books of original monologues, were chosen—along with *Creating Your Own Monologue, Promoting Your Acting Career, The Job Book,* and *The Job Book 2*—as "Featured Selections" in the Doubleday Book Club (Fireside Theater / Stage and Screen Division). Most of his published works have gone on to multiple printings.

As a playwright, Mr. Alterman is the recipient of the first Julio T. Nunez Artist's Grant, the Arts and Letters Award in Drama, and scores of playwriting awards, including being a three-time finalist at the Actors Theatre of Louisville Ten-Minute Play Competition.

His play *The Pain in the Poetry* was collected in *2009: The Best Ten-Minute Plays for Two or More Actors* (Smith & Kraus) and published by Playscripts.

His play *After* was published in *The Best Ten-Minute Plays of 2011* (Smith & Kraus), and his latest ten-minute play, *Second Tiers*, appears in *2012: The Best 10-Minute Plays* (Smith & Kraus).

Mr. Alterman's plays *Like Family* and *The Pecking Order* were optioned by Red Eye Films (with Alterman writing the screenplay). His play *Solace* was produced Off-Broadway by the Circle East Theater Company (formerly Circle Rep Theater Company). *Nobody's Flood* won the Bloomington National Playwriting Competition and was a finalist in the Key West Playwriting Competition.

Coulda-Woulda-Shoulda won the Three Genres Playwriting Competition two years in a row. The prize included publication of the play in a Prentice Hall textbook used in college theater departments all over the country.

Mr. Alterman wrote the book for *Heart Strings: The National Tour* (commissioned by DIFFA, the Design Industries Foundation for AIDS), a thirty-five-city tour that starred Michelle Pfeiffer, Ron Silver, Susan Sarandon, Marlo Thomas, and Sandy Duncan. Other plays include *Kiss Me When It's Over* (commissioned by E. Weissman Productions), starring and directed by André De Shields; *Tourists of the Mindfield* (finalist in the L. Arnold Weissberger Playwriting Competition at New Dramatists); and *Street Talk/Uptown* (based on his monologue books), produced at the West Coast Ensemble.

Goin' Round on Rock Solid Ground and *Unfamiliar Faces* were finalists at the Actors Theatre of Louisville's playwriting competition. *Spilt Milk* received its premiere at the Beverly Hills Rep/Theater 40 in Los Angeles and was selected to participate in the Samuel French One-Act Festival. *The Danger of Strangers* won Honorable Mention in the Deep South Writers Conference Competition, was a finalist in the George R. Kernodle Contest, was selected to be in the Pittsburgh New Works Festival, and has had over 35 productions, including at Circle Rep Lab, the West Bank Downstairs Theater Bar (starring James Gandolfini), the Emerging Artists Theater Company's one-act marathon, the Vital Theater Company in New York, and, most recently, with the Workshop Theater Company. There have been several major productions of his original monologues play, *God in Bed*, both in the United States and in Europe.

Mr. Alterman's work has been performed at Primary Stages, Ensemble Studio Theater (EST), Circle in the Square Downtown, HERE, LaMaMa, in the Turnip Festival, at the Duplex, at Playwrights Horizons, at several theaters on Theater Row in New York, and at many theaters around the country.

Mr. Alterman has been a guest artist and given master classes and seminars on monologues and the business of acting at such diverse places as the Governor's School for the Arts in Norfolk, Virginia; the Edward Albee Theater Conference (Valdez, Alaska); Southampton College; Western Connecticut State College; Broadway Artists Alliance; the American Federation of Television and Radio Artists (AFTRA), the Dramatists Guild; the Learning Annex; the Screen Actors Guild; the Seminar Center; in the Boston public school system; and at many acting schools and colleges all over the country.

In 1993, Mr. Alterman created the Glenn Alterman Studio, where actors receive monologue/audition coaching as well as career preparation. He was named "Best Monologue/Audition Coach in the Tri-State Area" by *Theater Resources Magazine* and first runner up as "The Best Private Acting Coach in New York" by the readers of *Back Stage*. He presently lives in New York City, where he's finishing his twenty-fifth book, tentatively titled *Monologues for Every Audition* (Smith & Kraus), and several new plays; coaching actors; and occasionally freelancing for film companies in the acquisitions department, helping turn plays into movies.

On the Web, he can be reached at www.glennalterman.com.